Andrew Griffin

From traditional to rational Faith

Or, The way I came from Baptist to liberal Christianity

Andrew Griffin

From traditional to rational Faith
Or, The way I came from Baptist to liberal Christianity

ISBN/EAN: 9783337167554

Printed in Europe, USA, Canada, Australia, Japan

Cover: Foto ©ninafisch / pixelio.de

More available books at **www.hansebooks.com**

From Traditional to Rational Faith;

OR,

THE WAY I CAME FROM BAPTIST TO LIBERAL CHRISTIANITY.

By R. ANDREW GRIFFIN.

BOSTON:
ROBERTS BROTHERS.
1877.

PREFACE.

AFTER much hesitation, this memoir is published. It is most painful to the author to say aught which reflects on that denomination whose kindness and love he has known from childhood. Yet, on all hands, so much astonishment is expressed that one living so long in the remote interior of orthodoxy should have rested at last in the Unitarian fellowship, that it may be desirable and of interest to give an account of the course pursued.

It is a matter of regret that the form of the story is intensely personal; but it was originally cast without any definite idea of publication, my chief anxiety being faithfully to record the exact impressions made from time to time.

I trust it may be useful to many who are struggling after the same manner. As it may fall into the hands of my English friends, whose letters full of Christian tenderness and undisguised anxiety have reached me, assuming I have proven recreant to the very spirit of the truths I taught them, — let me say, for the last time, perhaps, — Let us be quiet. I go my way, sorrowfully, without you. In this world, no argument nor language available can perhaps convince you that God, Christ, atonement, faith, prayer, and the inward life are as real and holy to me now as when I labored among you. You cannot see this; nor could I have seen it, a few years ago. Still, I go the way you go, — treading the same spiritual path you tread. The same Eternal Goodness guides us all; but we are separated, and walk on side by side, not knowing we are near, — together in spirit, yet separated until death reunites us. Then hope bids me say: In a world of realities, — a world free from artless bigotry, of imaginary duties, of enthralment in the literal and external, — we shall meet again, and Christ will neither spurn you nor me.

R. Andrew Griffin.

Marlboro', Mass, 1877.

CONTENTS.

Chapter		Page
I.	Early Influences	9
II.	Unrest	41
III.	Review of Church History	77
IV.	The Scriptures	121
V.	I. How I found him	145
	II. What he is to me	159
VI.	Temptation	175
VII.	Rest and Re-equipment	201

EARLY INFLUENCES.

" As is the world on the banks
So is the mind of the man
. . . . .
Only the tract where he sails
He wots of : only the thoughts
Raised by the objects he passes are his." ·
       MATTHEW ARNOLD.

FROM TRADITIONAL TO RATIONAL FAITH.

CHAPTER I.

EARLY INFLUENCES.

IN early childhood, I was familiar with evangelical religion in its most attractive and venerable forms. It was my good fortune to be reared by those whose sincerity and piety were beyond doubt. From the pulpit the prevailing type of orthodox belief was expressed in the least offensive way, and was permeated with what experience indorses as the essential ideas of rational faith. The preacher was politically a dissenter, and ecclesiastically a pronounced Baptist; but in the capacity of pastor and teacher he ascended from the conventional and sectarian, joining the ranks of those who, speaking in whatever theological tongue, declare the same eternal truths. The essential ideas of his teaching were the paramount importance of inward purity and loyalty to the truth: every thing was subordinated to these. Calvinism was as the light-house, — these constituted the light. And now, as one thinks of the structure, grim and antiquated, my gratitude is as deep as ever for the bright, clear light which, from then till now, has guided me on the sea of life, and wish intensely that he to whom I owe so much could see that, in rejecting the philosophy and theology of Augustine and Calvin, I do not, therefore, reject these truths he taught by means of their systems. The character of the instruction of those days may be judged from the following extracts. Words similar and ideas identical were the burden of what I heard from the first : —

"If there is no brokenness of heart, no conviction of mind, no trustful love, no adoring holiness, there is nothing the Creator has required or will accept. All that He will honor may be as readily found in the hovel as in the palace; in the barn as in the cathedral."[1]

Of the religion of Jesus: "It consisted not in forms and ceremonies in which no part of our nature, but our body, is necessarily engaged; nor in theories and creeds, which may dwell merely in the memory and on the tongue; nor in signs and wonders which may startle and

---

[1] "The Excellent Glory." John Aldis.

confound, but can never convince nor sanctify. It was the empire of truth in the mind, of law in the conscience, of love in the affections, and of holiness in the life, — a spiritual dominion, — the reign of God. These are the only treasures wherewith Christ will enrich us; these the only honors with which he will exalt us; and these the only delights with which he will gladden us."

"It set up the kingdom of God in the heart, and taught that the external was nothing except as it was related to the spiritual; that riches, honors, intelligence, and pleasures are nothing worth, unless the heart is right with God, but will rather prove the sources of guilt and misery. . . . It identified all true life and happiness with the love of God. It thus stimulated activity and brought repose; it cleansed the heart, and thus strengthened it; it taught men to worship the Most High, and to bless the poorest and guiltiest of men."

"The whole work of redeeming mercy aims at our sanctification."

"*Holiness* is *health*, — the being *whole*, spiritual soundness in the entire man."

"The kingdom of God is holiness and joy."[1]

[1] "The Excellent Glory." John Aldis.

"'By their fruits ye shall know them.' Orthodoxy may stand in solitude before the dread tribunal of the final judgment, and make its boast of a creed which, through life, furnished the excuse of indolence and the aliment of pride. It will be quite enough for the man of humility and faith to stand there and say, pointing to those he taught to seek after God, 'Here am I, and the children thou hast given me;' men who, in the essentials of Christian character, and in the energies of true devotedness to God; men who, in reaping the results of pious effort, and in evincing intimate friendship with the Saviour, have been excelled by none, — cannot be expected to stand, asking the sympathy of their fellows." [1]

The divine seed was sown, mixed with the adulterations of human mistakes, as, indeed, it always is, to some extent: but this was not all; the enemy sowed tares. Very early I can remember the influence of that class (found in every sect), who would dwarf the noblest forms of truth to fit the procrustean bed of their ignorant prejudice, and that of the denominational spirit, which sweeps over the nobler teaching of the prophets, as desert sands obliterate the

[1] "Lectures on Christian Union." John Aldis.

noblest cities of the plain. I learned, as most people do, to affect belief in the popular theology; professed, as a matter of course, all that those around me professed, and went on learning all that was taught on religious subjects, just as I learned the peculiar dialect of the English tongue spoken in my native county. All that I have since found to be illogical, legendary, and irrational, were sacred then. Just as a Hindoo child, reared by pious relatives and devout priests, bows within the temple of his native town, and never sees in its monstrous idols revolting spectacles; never connects with their many faces and many arms, bearing, as they do, murderous weapons and ghastly skulls, the ideas which occur of necessity to us.

One has often exclaimed, in one form or another, "O sancta simplicitas! O holy garden of Eden! where savage creatures were caressed as innocent companions; where poisoned berries were gathered and held in utter ignorance of their subtle and dangerous qualities. How great the misfortune, to be cast out from all this sweetness and unconscious bigotry, and how inconsiderable the fault of eating of the tree of polemics at the instance, not of a serpent, in view of self-exaltation, but when its fruit was pointed out by revered hands, and all men were bidden to eat in God's name and to his honor! The Baptist and Apostolic churches were regarded as identical in spirit and doctrine; every promise of the final triumph of Christianity meant the ultimate prevalence, if not of the sect, of its views. Divine favor rested on us because we were faithful to the truth above all others, and were conspicuous for the chivalry with which we asserted the simple right of private judgment. The historic church was Goliath; the conquering David was our communion together with the other dissenting denominations and the evangelical party in the Anglican Church; although these were regarded rather as sympathizing spectators than as the active and intimate companions of our arms,— the Lord's anointed, but as Saul was when David fought the Philistines.

As an English dissenter, and especially as "a dissenter of dissenters," as we called ourselves, I have had much less to unlearn and to trammel me than many who have fled from the captivity of traditional faiths. From the first we were inured to disregard of giants, magnitudes, antiquity, splendid ceremonials, majorities, saintly appearances,— these were spoken of as advantages which might be on the side of the most corrupt and pernicious religions. We were warned that these things ought not to carry any weight whatever in deciding between truth and error, right and wrong. Christ, exposed in loneliness and infamy, was pointed to as an all-sufficient proof that the divinest character and ideas might be associated with obloquy, scorn, minorities, ill-repute, and the charges of individualism, novelty, and, indeed, of blasphemy.

We saw in our feeble, oft-persecuted, socially despised sect Christ, in the servant form, doing battle again with the powers of ecclesiasticism and darkness. We were reminded that great historic names were associated as much with errors as truths; that even the reformers to whom we owed most were far from infallible. In the words of my pastor: "Unless the Protestant leaders had absolute infallibility, they could not have discovered 'the whole truth, and nothing but the truth.' As their opinions are corrected, therefore, new reformers must arise, to be cast off by them as they were cast off by Rome." The spirit of fearless inquiry and individual responsibility in matters of doctrine were insisted on: "Where there is no inquiry, a seeming unity will be preserved; and, where there is the power of oppression, differences may not be expressed; but where there is knowledge and freedom they are inevitable. The latitudinarian and hypocritical may remain quiescent; but the sincere and earnest will cheerfully bear the opprobrium of separation, if they feel they are approved of God. If unity is to be promoted, we must all abandon our assumed authority. The right to judge another man's conscience, or shape his creed, or sway his conduct, must never be claimed." [1]

Christ was declared to be the only final authority in matters of faith: neither churches nor councils nor reformers, however august and powerful, however illustrious the service they had rendered mankind or numerous their adherents, should come between us and him. That it was our solemn duty to ignore the lapse of time and in his immediate presence test all creeds and rites, that it behooved us to hear his word and imitate his example as though we were his contemporaries, to quote again from "Lectures on Christian Union:" "We have spoken freely of the Reformers and others; but let us not be suspected of indifference or disrespect. They were men of the divinest sort, whose 'shoes' latchet we are not worthy to loose.' Yet they

[1] "Lectures on Christian Union." John Aldis.

were but men, and they occupy a wrong place if ever they come between us and our Master. They did a great work. Doubtless the Spirit of God prompted and guided them. But they were fettered by circumstances, perhaps by prejudice and limited information. They must not give law to the Church ; for they themselves are under the law to Christ. Though of men they were the greatest, still they were but men." [1]

Every thing deemed essential Christian teaching was sought and professedly found in the sayings of Jesus. Modern theologies were projected into the first century, and hopelessly mixed together with primitive ideas. It was even held that Jesus taught the same doctrine of justification by faith in his vicarious and substitutionary work as Evangelicals do now. That when Christ declared " He that believeth and is baptized shall be saved," he virtually said, " You my mother, my brothers, my countrymen, unless you believe in my prospective death as the means whereby God, the first person of that Trinity of which I am the second person, will be able to save you from perdition, you cannot be saved from future misery at all nor brought in this life to a state of reconciliation with Him."

[1] "Lectures on Christian Union." John Aldis.

It was maintained by the most intelligent that the New Testament contained no such thing as a creed. "Had the New Testament furnished a creed it might have been convenient, certainly it would have been authoritative; but it has not."[1] Their idea of a creed is not a statement of doctrine, but a restatement of Biblical teaching. The letter of Scripture was confounded with its spirit in polemical encounters, and the Evangelical conception of its theology was not distinguished from the absolute truth. Yet, with the Socinian at a safe distance, in hours of special insight, my revered teacher at least evinced no inconsiderable appreciation of the great philosophical distinction between truth and its expression. While on the one hand he would say evangelical doctrines were infallible truth, on the other he gave utterance to such declarations as this: "How is the atonement effected? What precise end is answered by the death of Christ? The reply to this question is supposed to express the man's idea of the atonement. Yet how different are the notions of good men on this point. One has no idea but of a sacrifice; he sees in the victim of Calvary 'the Lamb of God,' and in his death the immolation of the

[1] "Lectures on Christian Union." John Aldis.

one offering which comprehended and superseded all others. Beyond this his thoughts never range. Another man fastens on the idea of redemption; he can think of nothing but the exchanges of the market; he sees that a price was demanded for the liberty of the captive, — not 'silver and gold' but the 'precious blood' of the Redeemer, — and he can view the death of Christ in no other light. A third party regards it in the light of law. With them the atonement is a legal expedient, by which the import of the law is more fully explained, and the authority of the divine government and character is vindicated and enforced, while the offender is forgiven and received into favor. We sometimes hear hard words applied to each other by the advocates of these several views, as giving mean and inadequate or unscriptural and heartless representations of the greatest theme of the evangelical economy. But really all these representations are furnished by the Scriptures; and the fault lies not in maintaining either, but in doing so by overlooking or rejecting all the rest. For, after all, it would appear that these are only figurative illustrations of great abstract principles of which without them we could form no conception whatever. . . . It is impossible, even if you employ the very words of the Bible, always to communicate the same ideas to different minds."[1] What would Mr. Spurgeon or Mr. Moody say to "the sacrifice of the cross" being a figurative expression in these days when "salvation by the blood" means salvation by the very physical blood-shedding of Jesus?

I could not at that time perceive the contradictory nature of the Protestant position as reflected in these discourses. Its higher precepts sank into my heart an abiding blessing, but its Evangelical theories captured my imagination, and gave me over for years to the reign of spiritual terror. Nevertheless, this early teaching, as a whole, has been of inestimable value in the struggle for fuller light and liberty. It seems, in retrospect, like the light of day, shining through dense clouds from which I passed into the dimmer light of a temple, a light casting weird shadows from stained windows and mysterious architecture, gradually fading away until one is left alone with nothing but the distant glimmer of altar lights; or, in plain words, rational ideas grew less and less distinct, and all that remained was the poor magic theology of modern revivalism. So great a difference is there between much of

[1] "Lectures on Christian Union." John Aldis.

the teaching of Robert Hall, J. H. Hinton, and John Aldis, and that of more popular but less gifted leaders of the sect to-day. In their presence it is evident I have but done as they have bidden, — logically applied the sounder principles of the faith, and pressed to legitimate conclusions the arguments they admitted. For by the same principle we have a right to decide for ourselves, without regard to the authority of Greek and Roman Christianity, we have an equal right to decide for ourselves without regard to them or any Protestant authority. If it be admissible to differ on grave subjects from Saint Augustine or Saint Athanasius, it is also admissible to differ on as grave subjects from Robert Hall or Andrew Fuller. If I when a mere lad could, with propriety, assert my own reason in presence of the venerable Grecian Fathers and all the Christian doctors of the last fifteen hundred years, it would not be presumptuous to think for myself at the feet of Protestant theologians.

The holiest, wisest, and most gifted religious guides I had known, in all sincerity and earnestness, bade me take the New Testament and study its contents as though no man nor church had defined its doctrines, and built upon them the inferential structures we call theology; that the spirit of truth would teach its fullest and deepest meanings to the plain, untheologic mind; that, without commentary or preacher, the simple and unsophisticated would arrive at Evangelical and Baptist conclusions; that if all other literature and churches were practically not in existence, the light of heaven would shine unimpaired from the Gospels and Epistles. I solemnly and fervently believed until but a few years ago, that the reason why all men were not Baptists was because the Pedobaptists deluded them by crafty explanations and spurious glosses; that all men were not Calvinists because they could not, or would not, hear for themselves the instructions of the sacred Scriptures.

Thus educated, what could one possessed of ordinary intelligence, and the spirit of honest inquiry do but end in a rational faith? The Denomination said, "Your reason is reliable enough to decide the nature of Baptism in face of all the priests and theologians who differ from us." It said, with unmistakable gravity, "Pass on; past the learned and the holy; past the venerable and exalted; past thrones of bishops and ranks of hierarchs; do not be abashed by their presence, their numbers, their arguments, their frowns, their menaces, their taunts, — boy, novice, uncritical as you are, you are qualified in this matter to think for yourself, to wave away all literature but the New Testament, and to arrive at a decision radically different from that of all Christendom.

Indeed, I can never forget the debt of gratitude I owe to a large portion of Baptist teaching. While it would have imposed its own theologic fetters, it snapped far heavier and more securely riveted chains. While it is wrathful because I bring a different report of ante-ecclesiastical Christianity, it showed the way to the past. While it bade me be faithful to its Calvinism, it also taught the great verities of rational godliness, and the fundamental principles of religious liberty.

For wellnigh twenty years, fascination and fear held me fast to its theological notions. Ignorance of the history of doctrines and of the church rendered me content with its creed. Its confusion, crudeness, and incomprehensibility were explained as the result of the intellectual feebleness of the human race. In these pages, I think it will be made clear that Baptist principles vanquished Baptist theology; and the influence of rational teaching, after lying for a long time in abeyance, cast out what was erroneous and immoral.

Indeed, I am a Unitarian *because* I was a Baptist; because faithful to those sacred principles without which the denomination had never come into existence; because I have not permitted it to be the arbiter of my theological opinions, — a function which it affirmed no church had the right to assume.

Nor do I despair of the day when the denomination shall emancipate its own principles and opinions from the tyrannical control of superstition. There are reasons to hope its more philosophical and scholarly members have little sympathy with the sectarianism and theological crudities characteristic of its present condition. As the writer already quoted remarks of denominationalism: "Denominationalism is raised above the Christian name. He who bears not the former is looked upon with suspicion, or dislike, as wofully ignorant or singularly perverse. He may be well attested, as adorned by all those graces which are inseparable from the love of the truth and a holy life; but he does not inspire confidence, for he hears our most talismanic words with an apathy which is not only strange but repulsive. Another man bears the distinctive name. It is not known that he is assimilated to the Saviour; nay, it might be easily discovered, that he is very slenderly imbued with vital godliness; but he repeats the password, and rushes at once into the sanctuary of our love. We are insensible to the extent of this evil, only because we are so familiar with it. It is this which fosters exclusiveness of intercourse and uncharitableness of spirit; which induces us to impugn the motives and arraign the conduct of good men; which chills our sympathies and narrows our benevolence; and in their place creates or discovers the elements of estrangement and war."[1]

Of the theologic spirit he writes: "How strange it is, that Christians should so much more frequently separate from each other on account of difference of sentiment, than on account of difference of character! How much more repulsive are diverse religious observances than unhallowed tempers; how much sooner do we suspect the indications of heterodoxy than the risings of sin! . . . How is it our moral infirmities are mutually tolerated? It is supposed that they are compatible with a true Christian character. . . . We ask that the same line of

[1] "Lectures on Christian Union." John Aldis.

conduct only, should be pursued in regard to differences of theological belief and ritual observance."[1]

As I grew up I came to regard righteousness as a very different thing from right being and right doing; it was rather agreement with the thought and obedience to the requirements of a supermundane being whether according to my mind his thought was error or truth, his requirements moral or immoral. As it now appears, I was tempted to turn a deaf ear to God's voice speaking through reason and conscience, heeding implicitly what an imaginary being was supposed to believe and command by a portion of mankind who have notoriously erred in their speculations, and the best of whom were fallible men, as they would have themselves confessed. The Calvinistic conception of God robbed of its meaning all the healthful teaching of which illustrations have been given; *virtue* no longer meant loyalty to conscience, but subservience to one's betters; *loyalty to truth* no longer signified fidelity to the necessary convictions of the mind; *love of God* ceased to be devoted affection for *The best*, it became feudal attachment to a Master. This conception overawed and paralyzed

[1] "Lectures on Christian Union." John Aldis.

alike the intellect and heart, blighted all enjoyment and peace. I was an anxious Servetus afraid to do wrong, because the stern eyes of an irresponsible Calvin in the skies pursued me everywhere, with hands clenched in threatening ready to smite down to everlasting fires if we offended, ready to relax and caress in a cold official way if we pleased. I gave myself to all sorts of rigors. Mirth was folly, and comfort sin. No day was tolerable without self-inflicted misery. It seemed a duty to eat little and that of the plainest, and do nothing except with the demurest air. No monk ever rose from penance with more satisfaction. If taught to worship my mother, I had drawn nearer to God than worshipping the mental image thus called by His Holy name. Gratefully I remember the influence of Christ in those days. The dreamy thought was a solace, that, in some way or other he was God, and as in dreams one's ideas run together, clash, are metamorphosed into all sorts of strange juxtapositions and shapes, so I thought of Jesus. Now his hands were bleeding and transfixed in self-sacrificing love, then extended in imperious gestures; now he was the merciful friend, then the fierce, austere taskmaster who hereafter would combine with his Father against offenders, making heaven echo with his derisive laughter at the agonies and discomfiture of his foes. Still the idea of Christ was mainly associated with tenderness, goodness, forgiveness. Indeed, as long as Christendom has its immoral, vindictive ideal of the Deity, surely it is a question whether the fictions of a celestial Mary and Jesus are not so beneficent that a devout heart might pray for their continuance wherever there is no prospect of emancipation from mediæval horror.

I learned to relegate every thing irrational and unintelligible to the shades of mystery, and justified every thing revolting to my moral sense as right because God had willed it.

The thought of man utterly ruined, outlawed, cursed, doomed to ever-continuing woe in another world, because he would not, and could not, obey God; the thought, a given number were elected to virtue and fortune irrespective of their own efforts; the thought, God had contrived the crucifixion on purpose to honor his justice; the thought, God was ever taking note of all inattentions, misbeliefs, and mistakes,— while they rendered me most unhappy and perplexed, were cherished as integral parts of "the glorious Gospel;" and a despicable kind of relief was found in some moods, from the reflection, — whatever the rigors and anomalies of the Divine government, I had believed, had striven to do right, had repented, and therefore was of the number of the elect, and hereafter would be so constituted as to hear the shrieks of lost souls, though they were my brothers, only to turn with admiring eyes to the contemplation of the perfections of God.

But there was always the secret misgiving of self-deception, of defective belief. At the same time we were taught to labor for the salvation of men as though there were no such fact as the election of some; to be as active to proclaim the goodness of God as though all could be saved. It seemed most irrational to educate men for the ministry, except so far as was necessary for the repetition of "the saving truths of the Gospel." I marvelled men should be taught the various branches of learning; of what use was it to study the Greek and Latin classics, mathematics, and history? Why the endeavor to make ministers cultured gentlemen? Why the grasping at the honors of "carnal knowledge!" Did not every Christian know all that was necessary to salvation? Did it matter how this was communicated, or by whom; for was it not the power of God? Was not the race perishing with every breath we drew, and is not our one business in life to preach the Gospel so that the elect may be gathered to the fold, and the non-elect left without excuse? Should firemen be calmly trained while houses are burning? Should recruits pass through the curriculum of cadets when war is at the door? Gradually the idea of election receded, and the doctrine of human responsibility came to the front. Revivalism breathed its feverish breath into the bones of Calvinism.

About this time, Mr. Spurgeon had obtained a denominational reputation. His personal excellences, his rhetorical ability, but, above all, his evangelical earnestness, fascinated the unofficial and unfastidious portions of every church. I leave hostile critics, and those unconnected by personal ties of affection and gratitude to say all that can be said in disparagement of him, or of the movement he helped to originate. None who know him and his work can doubt his sincerity, his ability, his devotedness, nor his philanthropy; and in all candor we may record the belief that were he a clergyman of the Anglican Church, or a leader among rational Christians, he would be as famous and as useful. He started by accepting the average theological ideas of the Baptists. I should say they were never seriously questioned. He never fought to gain, but only to retain, his belief. Familiar from childhood with real piety and practical goodness in those holding these views, he naturally attributed their religious life to their theological opinions. But, while impressed with the beauty and necessity of holy living, he was more attracted by the thought of the millions who were doomed to endless woe, unless they believed in Jesus Christ. He devoted himself, as every humane man of his opinions ought. He believed intensely what the more refined decorously affirmed they believed. The latter admitted the most awful things of Calvinism to their creed. Man utterly ruined without the power of self-help; God able only to save him from future calamity in one way; that in the Christian preacher is invested the power whereby the helping hand of God is brought down to the supplicating hand of man; that on his earnestness and faithful presentation of the divine message hangs the destiny of those who hear him. To him God is as a mighty sovereign, whose smile is sunlight to his lieges, whose frown is despair and death; a being whose generosity to his favorites is as lavish as his severities to offenders are cruel. He believed all that. He believed it as the theological *littérateur*, as the average place-seeking pastor, the respectable worldly church-member, never can. His pulse beat in unison with that of the common-sense masses, who know nothing of comparative theology, who believe they have under their arms, in the Bible carried there, a talismanic remedy for sin, and a magic preventive of eternal misery, — the masses who had said to cold propriety, to orthodox self-satisfaction, to prosperous pietism, "If you believe souls are perishing, and you have the means of saving them, why don't *you do something?*" Spurgeon was their ideal. He affirmed the current views. Say, if we will, he dragged into the light the old Juggernaut: but it had not been there to drag out, if the scholarly had *said their esoteric thoughts; or it had been dragged out before if they had none.*

He did and said what simple-minded people feel ought to be the course and language of one who really believed what they had been taught was infallible truth. At that time he gave language to what had before been shaping itself in my own mind, and fixed in my imagination those conceptions of God and of Christ, and of the Baptist form of Evangelical dogmatics in general, which held in abeyance the more rational and healthful teaching I had received. Nor can I ever regret the fervor with which I followed him. To believe in the Evangelical theory, and lack zeal, is inhumanity.

I commenced my ministry in a society which in point of intelligence and piety, I should say would compare favorably with any church of whatever name. The members had imbibed the taste for revivalism, but retained the habits of conservatism. They expected the enthusiasm which can only be influential when contagious. The more earnest spirits deplored their lack of piety because they could not rise to the elevation of feeling and intensity of concern which they believed should mark them as men saved amid those respited, yet unrepentant. They and I expected all the physiological and psychological phenomena possible only among large audiences under the spell of electrical oratory, or in the presence of public calamities. Yet there was a sound substratum of healthy religious sentiment. The appeal to terror, the artifices of vulgar propagandisms, were distasteful. They were children longing for the wild excitements of frenzied crowds, yet conscious of the happiness of home, and industrious there; trying to act concerning God and men, as though he was a tyrant, and they his victims, and yet held back by an unrecognized consciousness of his goodness, which neutralized their theological misrepresentations.

Men seemed to me culpably patient. As I viewed the world, its condition was more heart-rending than Egypt with the plague and death in every home and stall. As I view those English homes from *my present stand-point*, I feel how natural and beautiful they were; as I saw them *then*, peace was guilty indolence, unostentatious piety was spiritual selfishness and decorous indifference, orderly public worship was a feeble substitute for impassioned supplication of God and frenzied appeals to souls in utmost peril. Both in my first and second charge I felt the same oppressive sense of the impossibility of maintaining a temper consistent with such a creed as ours. I strove to lash myself into a fervid state, now blaming others, then blaming myself: there had not been prayerfulness enough in private, or faithfulness enough in the pulpit, or the congregation lacked enthusiasm. Whatever the cause, I was mournfully convinced of the uninfluential character of our religious opinions; and noticed, in proportion as men were of a cultured and robust manhood, they preferred the suppression of Calvinistic and Baptist crudities. Of course, none said it in so many words; nobody would have thought of denying one of these tenets: for men cherish the name of orthodoxy when they have long abandoned the thing. But it could be seen, clearly enough, that they did not, for example, believe in everlasting punishment for all unbelievers. One thinks of those bright Sunday mornings,— the lovely bay, skirted with the white, English cliffs, and the clear, pure heavens without and above; the congregation of holiday visitors and well-to-do residents of the town seated within, in their Sunday best; their fair, bright girls and boys beside them,— and knows, when the conviction was most strenuously resisted, they did not, could not, believe that He who had made the world without could really speak through me the ghastly doctrine, that all those hoydens and youths, those matrons and men of the world, were condemned culprits before Him, who, unless they believed my theology with all their hearts, must every one go down for evermore to a scene of woe worse than dungeons, scaffolds, hospitals, or star-chambers ever witnessed. I thought I believed it, — thought I was doing God service in thrusting the revolting dogma between them and their present happiness ; but I see now it was believed as children believe a frenzied mother when she says, half beside herself with vexation, that, unless they are obedient, she will whip them to death ; not as men believe in the death-sentence from the lips of an implacable and irresponsible judge. God has so made us that we cannot possibly think as ill of him as we try. When I stood by the dead, — the early dead, who living had never professed conversion, nor subscribed to any article of religious faith, — the thought constantly arose, Could a man, however rigid and hard his professed opinions, dare approach the corpse and say, " If she whose remains lie here before us, — she who was kind to all, whose beauty touched our hearts and won our love, and whose sweetness of nature lingers still in the expression of that dead face, — if she did not believe what we believe, and think and feel concerning God as we do, her young soul is now in the extremest suffering, and hereafter that body shall rise to express for evermore agonies as awful as her soul can know." No man, one's better nature insisted, could say that, if his nature was purged from brutality ; no man could really *think it*, and pray; no man could believe that, and believe also *conscience* as well as *power* was in God. But all such relenting thoughts were dismissed as suggestions of the Devil, or as the promptings of the spirit of self-deception, too timid or kind to admit the worst. I thought of myself as a false prophet, ready to heal the hurt slightly, and quenched the light of reason with the sacred extinguisher never far from the priest's fingers. I said, " It is the truth of God; I am his messenger; the consequences are with him." I tried to show the goodness of God in forewarning men, and regarded the presence of such repulsive ideas in the Gospel as proof of its divine origin; for I reasoned, men would never have imagined a future so humiliating and terrible for themselves. I did not think at that time how men had been busy from the beginning in inventing racks, thumbscrews, brazen bulls, guillotines, cannons, torpedoes;— that one portion of mankind had industriously sought to render the other portion miserable, even when it was more than likely the persecutor might find himself the victim of his own designs.

Moreover, I was convinced, as I am now, that if the orthodox interpretation and the common theories of inspiration are true, it is absurd to question the gloomy and terrible teachings of the Bible, when we accept all beside.

From time to time the influence of the semi-rationalistic spirit breathed in general literature reached me: but if I shuddered at the logical consequences of Calvinism, I shuddered more at the possibility of free thinking; my sermons for years bear the proof of my rage against all I called latitudinarianism. I regarded the light of reason as the king in the drama feared the light of heaven for his blind daughter; or as the Roman prisoner, into whose dungeon penetrated but one ray of light, feared if the prison were demolished it would destroy that fissure, and thus deprive him of the priceless boon of light altogether.

UNREST.

"The great division among Christians is about opinions. Every sect has its set of them, and that is called orthodoxy; and he that professes his assent to them, though with an implicit faith, and without examining them, is orthodox, and in the way of salvation. But if he examines, and thereupon questions, any one of them, he is presently suspected of heresy; and if he oppose them, and hold the contrary, he is presently condemned as in a damnable error, and in the sure way to perdition." — JOHN LOCKE.

CHAPTER II.

UNREST.

IN May, 1871, I came to the United States. That journey was the first stage toward the liberal faith, though unconsciously taken. It did not appear, till long after, how destructive a shock my religious opinions had received, nor the name by which men indicate that which I experienced, nor the results they suggested. It was in the nature of a painful surprise, that men had labelled and exhibited, applauded or derided, these things; calling them "mystical sentiment," "free thinking," "transcendentalism," "rationalism." To me it was the listening to a voice nought within challenged; it was the speech of facts, realities chasing prejudices and impossible errors, — the voice of God! The experience was too painful, startling, confusing. The world whirled, the stablest things grew frail, the very "mountains flowed." As my native land receded, as home, friends, church, faded in the distance, — left alone,

— the question pressed, What is life? What does matter *mean*? Is there not more than semblance between the phantasmagoria of a dream and the changing scenes of life? Is the outer world a more perfect dream, and self a more unconscious dreamer? Are ideas as much facts as things? Why not? If aught is, in whatever realm of existence, is it not a *fact*, a *reality*? We can say of a stone, it is; we can say with equal emphasis of a dream-stone, it *is*, — the one within, the other without. May it not be an infirmity of ours to call the one real and the other unreal? Men of a lower order call meats and drinks and animal indulgences the solid realities; but those of a nobler nature call the unseen qualities of virtue and truth realities, and the things of sense transient and illusory. May it not be that it is we who determine the nature of things: that the outer world is the rough picture of the inner; that we call the landscape, with its distances and shadowy outlines and changing hues and intangibility, the *ideal*, and the painting which we can touch, with its harder lines and unvarying hues, *reality?* And may it not be that this we call "sin" is the power which steals our higher consciousness; which isolates us from the great whole; which sends us to

sleep, and shuts us up to the dream we call life;
which is, in truth, only a parenthetical life, — real
as far as it goes, but sorrowful and disquieting
because of its confusions and limitations and
the indefinable sense we have lost something,
and are beguiled, like the dreamers within the
dream struggling to wake? And may not Death
be the going to ourselves, — to the whole; not
the loss of any thing, but the gain of all: so that
the holy things we call time-bound, transient,
local, provisional, may remain with us, disassociated from the ideas of time and size and form, —
reality stripped of the incomprehensible and
unreal; so that we shall lose the curiosity and
wonder, the critical habit and strangerhood, of
sight-seers, and become at last at home in the
Father's house, and go about our true business,
and enjoy our true relations?

Things cannot be what they seem. This sea,
this sky, — what does it all mean? The billows
heaving day after day; this sky, with its ever-changing and mysterious clouds, — what is at
the back of all? Nothing seems more real, and
nothing more unreal. When I think of the
solar system, — of stellar worlds, of space, and
of the unexplored beyond, and of the Inconceivable, as inconceivable, if limited as if unlim-

ited, — then this mighty sea and sky are no more to me than a stone to a child. Yet, in other moods, it is vast, awful; its tiniest animalcule as much affects me with wonder as the heights and depths and breadths and lengths of the universe. There is something which is not, which *ought to be*, which *may be*, — a something as natural, perhaps, as waking. My dreams are all subjective, *that is certain;* and as subjective when we think them objective as when we have no thought of their relation to mind or matter, — as when we are worldly and immersed in dreams, having no sense they are only dreams and no desire to awaken! What have I been doing in assuming to know so much about God, when his simplest works are inscrutable? What have I been doing in telling men, a mere handful as they are in comparison with the peoples of the earth, that God specially loves them because they think certain things, and feel, in certain moods and certain tenses, certain sensations? Might not the birds of one forest just as rationally believe that if they all tried to sing like the nightingale, and all believed the true song was its song, they should all secure God's love above other birds, and go, at death, to sing that same song in celestial groves; while other birds and beasts and fishes and men and women, who could not sing in that way, or could not sing at all, should suffer imprisonment in cruel hands, within cages of iron, unfed, unheeded?

What was our theology but one set of opinions among many? And what were our missionaries doing, perhaps, but trying to teach foreign birds our native song? And those who learned it, did they catch the sweetness of thought and life which these had to whom it came as an inheritance, and who were fitted by nature for it? Were not our proselytes and all proselytes thinking our thoughts as a parrot might imitate a nightingale's notes? And would it not be better to sing to them our song, and hear them sing their own, and hope that each might learn from each, and trust that God hears and approves us all? And then the oft-recurring thought came, — Do we really believe what we profess? We say we have "the Gospel," the only teaching which can bring these myriads into the divine favor, and save them from future and unending misery; and yet behind me are these men and women, who hold this awful possession, buying, selling, marrying, giving in marriage, feasting, sleeping, thronging their favorite preachers, striving like other men for wealth and place and precedence and power. Do they and I really believe that Gospel would save millions now living, and millions yet unborn; and yet no one man, save officials, do as much to spread its teachings as he does for his own personal and temporal comfort? Do they and I believe that the money spent in luxuries,—indeed, in much deemed necessities,—is the one thing needful to give that Gospel to thousands on thousands? And if they believed it as they believe a house is on fire, and were as heroic to save men as property,—what then? England would find in every Protestant, Calvinistic congregation a congregation of madmen. The simple instinct of humanity would lead men to strip off their very clothes, and swathe themselves in coarsest fabric, if the thought burned itself into the brain and heart: These clothes are worth five pounds; five pounds would give some heathen the Gospel; that Gospel would save him from misery worse than a million years in the Black Hole of Calcutta. Indeed, would it not be an awful curse if men really believed all the holiest have taught and the sincerest professed?

Then came thoughts of the old life: the piety, the dignity of character, the purity and peace, the intelligence and learning, the influence and age, of those who had led me in youth, who had taught me words of help and light, who had impressed me with the importance of divine things, — it could not be they were mistaken? I could not bear God's voice: it spoke of things so awful, of subjects so vast, of errors — if errors they were — so enormous and fatal. I would have run to Eli, and found refuge from the darkness and an answer for the voice. And, foolish as the exclamation is, one has said it in bitterness: "Would that all teachers of the truth were good men, and all teachers of error, bad!"

The vision passed. I persuaded myself it was a sinful indulgence in idle speculation, if not an outburst of impious scepticism; congratulated myself on having had one of those experiences which eminent saints had had, and should be able hereafter to speak of a triumph over the Devil, and say to thoughtful and anxious young men, "I have been where you have been, and know all about your difficulty. Do as I did: leave speculation, and believe."

But those hours of insight were not to be forgotten: they pursued me. I strove to shake them off as one does an impertinent hanger-on. I resolved to lay the spectres of the mind with devout vociferations and unremitting activities; engaged earnestly in the work of the propagandist; sought to become intensely sectarian; and assailed every form of anti-evangelical thought, as one who plunges into the thick of the fight, lest he should be tempted to espouse the cause of the enemy. This is recorded with much self-reproach; but it seems, in reviewing the past, I was sincere. But henceforth I was divided: the critic stood behind the dogmatist, and self-accusation waited on self-assertion. The measure meted to myself I dealt out to others; was keenly alive to the contradictions and confusions of thought which heretofore had passed unchallenged; and recoiled from methods of influencing men in favor of our faith, approved by even the wisest and the best.

The theological world was a Babel; and its mission, in the light of scientific facts, was analogous to the work of building a tower to reach (as we imagined in childhood of the Scripture story) the dome of heaven.

Its attitude toward Christ was now painfully humanitarian; then, as painfully idolatrous. Now he was spoken of as a Free Religionist would hesitate to speak; for example, "The waif of Bethlehem, the boy of Nazareth, the simple, young Judæan peasant."[1] Then it was

[1] Sermon of Rev. T. Armitage, in Annual Report of Bible and Publication Society, 1874.

said, "The trembling little hand which tangles its helpless fingers in the virgin mother's hair is the hand that fabricated orbits, and launched millions of worlds trooping through space." "Can you think of any *deficiency* in *Jesus Christ* that you could supply from the character of Jehovah himself, and that, supplied, would render him more perfect; or can you *remove from his character any redundancy* which would be unworthy of Jehovah, if it were transferred from the breast of Jesus to the breast of Jehovah?"[1]

Christ was at once the supreme Deity and a person with whom one could be exceedingly familiar. He was "our God" and our "dear Jesus." Greeted now with the veneration of a worshipper, then with the raptures of a lover. Ecce Homo at one time meant "Behold the Creator;" at another time, "Behold the first Baptist, an amiable person incapable of resenting the rudenesses of acknowledged partisans." Ministerial education was insisted on as an all-important preparation for the ministry; the profoundest scholarship was deemed an unmitigated blessing: yet, at the same time, nothing was to be viewed save from the denominational stand-point

[1] Ibid.

and through the denominational lens. Did not Rome say the same words, and mean the same thing?

It was asserted in good faith that we were true to the great principle of the Reformation, and eschewed authority in matters of faith altogether; every man was supposed to have formed his own creed, and his agreement with the denomination was a pure coincident: yet we combined, with all the energy we possessed, to cast odium upon all who did not conform to so insignificant a department of opinion as our close-communion views, and arraigned the open-communion organ as an indecent offender, because it bore our name and assumed to be a denominational paper. Like the tenant of a coffin, there was plenty of room if a man would only keep still. Much stress was laid on sacramental observance: the ordinance must be celebrated exactly as the New Testament was supposed to prescribe. Yet I knew that the New Testament mentioned no such formula as "In the name of the Father, the Son, and the Holy Ghost." It was required of the convert that he should profess belief "in his own personal justification by faith in the substitutionary work of Jesus." Of this I knew that the New Testament reports no such arrangement, but required belief in Jesus as the prophetic Messiah, or in his resurrection.

Of the Lord's Supper it was declared that every thing should be after the order of the night "in which he was betrayed." A hard line should be drawn at the last words of the book of Revelation, and our minds fixed on Jesus and that first celebration: there, and there only in the Gospels, was our pattern. Yet the rite was a *church* rite: we had looked in horror on any who should have kept "the feast" in their own houses. Yet I knew, that at first, that supper was celebrated without priest or clergyman, — a feast instituted by a layman, for laymen, in a private room.

We said, in good faith, "Preach the Gospel: nothing but it can save. Declare the whole counsel of God: man fallen, Christ incarnate, salvation through his blood, heaven and hell as the respective destinies of saint and sinner." And we preached total depravity, — told the children they were hopelessly lost, ruined, accursed; knowing that not one of us who professed to be "washed in the blood" had as few faults or as pure a heart as these children! And we preached salvation by sacrificial transfer. We said in other words what we could not translate into the vernacular of secular speech, except by such terms as these: "salvation by fiction;" "salvation by a human sacrifice;" "justice satisfied by injustice;" "Heaven propitiated by one who willed his own death, and permitted his executioners to incur the odium of murder and persecution, because of a private arrangement with the Deity of which the instruments of his death knew nothing." And yet intelligent men did not mean *that*. The popular preachers might, the uneducated might, the fanatical might; but they meant something very difficult of expression, requiring the greatest care and exactness on the part of the preacher, and more than ordinary acumen on the part of the hearer, and did not agree among themselves as to the essential idea of the doctrine. Here, then, was a dogma of speculative theology thrust on the people as an infallible truth, which they must believe, — *that itself;* not something like it, but the very dogma as the doctors held it, — or else they might miss the grace of God, and heaven at last. I reflected, whatever the truth or utility of the doctrine of the atonement, it surely requires to be known in its integrity as it is, and not a distorted rendering of it. An incorrect statement of speculative knowledge may be worse than no statement at all. What is the Socinian statement but a modification of the orthodox? It, too, points to Christ crucified; it, too, speaks of atoning merit; it bids men trust in Christ for salvation, and celebrates the glories of the atonement: yet Socinians, we held, were as far from God and salvation as atheists! Only a difference of theory and statement made the gulf. Yet who of the mass of evangelical preachers state the doctrine with precision? Have Socinians ever distorted it as our revivalists? Do untheologic Socinians know any less of the meaning of Christ's death, practically, than untheologic orthodox church-members? Is not all popular knowledge general, inexact, approximate? I felt sure we could select almost any lay member of our churches, and state any one of the theories of atonement, and he would not detect heresy. If I said to him, "The great end and purpose of our Lord's sufferings was to produce a divine effect upon our heart, so that we should loathe and leave sin, and thus be meetened for heaven," would he deny that? would that pass for error? Yet scientific theologians know that *that* is the deadly error of Socinians,— such a perversion of the truth that it is said "to make void the grace of God."

And of all the articles of our creed, the opinion was forced on me, the majority of the laity had as imperfect and vague a conception. While every one professed to believe in the orthodox doctrines of the trinity, of original sin, of justification, of redemption, of inspiration, it was evident very few could so express what they understood by the terms as to be in substantial accord with each other or with the standard statements of the denomination; that, if they stated their conception of these doctrines, a well-informed theologian could detect heresy darker than Arius or Socinus ever taught.

Surely, then, if salvation from destruction depended on theological teaching, — a kind of teaching requiring so much clearness of thought and expression, — the masses are at the mercy, to an alarming extent, of clergymen well-meaning, interesting, diligent, but wholly incapable of precision and lucidity of statement. Did they dispense arsenic, nux-vomica, or belladonna with the same lack of discrimination and carefulness as the Gospel remedy is preached, our families would be poisoned on all hands. In theology, as in medicine, extravagance may be fatal. Saying too much or too little, the use of a single word, the introduction of the nearest synonym, may transform our teaching into heresy.

Practically, I found speculative theology was little known or valued. Its names and terms were respected, quoted, treated as shibboleths; but the things themselves were not apprehended. I know it will be painful to beloved and honored friends to read this; but it is a deliberate and carefully formed opinion. Nor should they attribute so disparaging a judgment to the oblique vision of one who has left their fold. In the words of a writer whose orthodoxy has never been aspersed, and whose eminence has never been questioned, among English Baptists at least: "Take the extreme points of Calvinism and Arminianism, . . . there are multitudes who will proclaim and defend either doctrine who are alike deficient in serious thought and true piety. They have never meditated deeply, but repeat certain phrases which they but imperfectly understand and could not define at all. Yet their confidence is only measured by their ignorance. Their presumption is really frightful. They pronounce on the most awful topics as if they had gauged the infinite Mind, and sat in familiar intercourse by the throne of God. They regard themselves, and are regarded by others, as almost infallible; 'valiant for the truth' in a world of perfidious cowardice, and the luminaries of 'sound doctrine' in the midst of a worse than Egyptian darkness."[1] I do not go as far as this: I do not impute to religious "*multitudes*" this offensive self-conceit; that is, no doubt, true of a class distributed throughout almost all the churches. But I do say, "the multitudes" who profess to be saved by belief have no exact or intelligent conception of their creed; the attachment to names and phrases is out of all proportion to their knowledge of the doctrines they represent; practical piety exists independently of them; artificial creeds have little influence in improving character, — men are better than their creeds, full often, and good irrespective of them, as a general rule; that speculative theology flourishes nowhere but in the hot air of controversy, and is understood by few save professional men.

As converts were admitted to the church, it was clear they did not and could not be expected to understand the doctrines of the Society; that it required as much training and ability to learn the Baptist ideas concerning "the atonement" as to learn political doctrine or medical theories. Yet all who were received imagined they held the tenets of the sect so intelligently, and prized them so highly, that they could rank among be-

[1] "Lectures on Christian Union."

lievers, and would secure the everlasting benefits of correct theological views.

At those times when the fictitious and artificial are generally laid aside, — in severe trials, in sickness, in death, — I saw conspicuous evidence of how uninfluential this class of doctrine was. The one thought which gave support was the infinite love of God; and the one source of satisfaction was rectitude of character. The true sacramental wine for dying lips was not the residuum of polemics, but the blessed catholic hope of the charity of God. My whole being revolted from asking men and women, at such times, as to their literary agreement with my school of thought, and was forced to do as now, — point them to the hospitable arms of the Heavenly Father, whose compassion answered to their frailty, and whose mercy rested alike on the wise and the ignorant, the righteous and "the sinner that repented."

The impression deepened, that creeds had little to do, in the vast majority of cases, with righteousness in life or fortitude in death; the nature of the fatal disease had often more to do with the religious experience of the dying than their opinions. For every man who bemoaned, in the last hour, his neglect of church religion, there are those, whose ecclesiastical standing has been unimpeachable, who have sunk despairing into the grave, because they feared they had not believed aright after all, and had not experienced the kind and degree of spiritual life which would entitle them to the heavenly rest.

I have found the church has no monopoly of virtue; but in every community are those of the purest morality and the deepest religious sentiment, who habitually avoid all ecclesiastical observances, and who decline to profess agreement with any of the sectarian theologies.

I was convinced that the usual method of propagating our creed and increasing our membership was unfair and exceptional; that the clergy flippantly asserted inspiration, and assumed passing impressions of their own were the suggestions of the Eternal Spirit; that, under protection of their sacred character, they employed modes of persuasion no other profession would think of tolerating among their class. I imagined a barrister seeking to influence the mind of a jury on behalf, say, of a man accused of murder, whom he sincerely believed innocent, as clergymen seek to influence men on behalf of their technical dogmatics; telling them the Lord of justice desires them to return a verdict on behalf of his client, — he is sure of this, for he prayed over it; warning them not to reason on the matter, that reason was not infallible, and if they trusted to their intellects, if they hesitated under stress of his speech to decide, God might leave them to abiding scepticism, and they would never agree upon a verdict.

When I saw men rushing from a political meeting, excited by a great speech, declaring their views and sympathies entirely changed from one party and its doctrines to another, I asked myself, What evidence is there that religious opinions, accepted under similar circumstances, are of more value, or more likely to be occasioned by divine power? Was it not true that the great majority of proselytes were among the impressionable and ignorant; that the best members of our churches were those who had grown up under religious influences, and were Baptists just as a similar class are Lutherans or Presbyterians or Episcopalians, — because their denominational religion is their familiar, native faith? It was really chosen for them, and they see the good in it, and have come gradually to feel the ancestral sect is their spiritual home: a class who expect and covet the raptures of "conversion," that they may be like everybody else of their order; a class who, in a very large number of instances, never do nor can have this species of hysteria, and ever after are troubled lest "a work of grace" never took place in them.

It was perplexing to observe the common treatment of reason. Now it was appealed to as the final judge of truth; then it was impeached as an impertinence and a foe. We seemed to treat reason as some of the Italians do their wayside shrines. As they go to the lottery, they kneel and invoke the saints to aid them in drawing a lucky number; but, if they are unsuccessful, they pelt these same images as they return. So long as reason served our purpose, we deferred to it; but, when it challenged our opinions, we appealed to a something else we called faith. "Faith, what is it," I said, "but the dark closet where we thrust ugly questions and inconvenient arguments?" I thought much on the nature of reason, saw there was great confusion in the current conception of it. What was it but the power by which we know?—not simply the power by which we prove, but also the power by which we perceive. My reason teaches me two and two make four; by reason I know I am: but in neither case can I reason out why these things are so. I perceive by this inward sight God is that which is not man nor thing, small nor great; that which is all I am, but not what I am; the sum, and not the parts; of whom we can never say what we ought to say, without saying what we ought not. But it is not self-evident that God is a trinity in unity; because we cannot conceive of three in one and one in three, of the divided and united, at the same time.

If faith meant reason quickened by the divine spirit to clearer vision, then faith was another term for reason. But faith, as commonly understood, was really the power of submission to the unreasonable; the power of treating unknown things as though they were reasonable. I asked myself, Is not this, after all, but a way of piously shutting our eyes, and giving the priests the chance to dupe us? If we shut our eyes never so piously, and opened our mouth never so trustfully, how did we know who would take advantage of our condition? We were really saying to the people, You must believe what, in the nature of things, you cannot understand, and what we do not understand ourselves, and don't know anybody who does understand or has understood. As Robertson put it: "Now do you believe in *abracadabra?*" — "Sir, do you?" — "Yes." — "Then, so do I. But what is *abracadabra?*" — "Never mind that: we believe."

Many a weary month I pondered this question: "Was it required of us to believe because we were told a thing was true?" Was there some other arbiter of opinion beside the verifying faculty (as I learned afterward to call it)? Was not this truth-seeing gift the power of God in us? was it not the channel of inspiration? May we not see the truth as prophets express it, as truly as they did; and was not their special gift the power of intelligibly presenting their intuitions in thoughts and words? And can we be said to believe any truth we cannot thus see? If we say we accept all truth, known and unknown, perceived and unperceived, are we not juggling with words? And ought we not to say we believe what we see, and desire fuller knowledge?

Was not this implied in our great principle of the right of private judgment? All was confusion. It was our duty to submit to the authority of the Scriptures; yet it was also our duty to judge the Scriptures were authoritative. Man was too ignorant to decide on its contents in detail; yet he must decide the whole was infallible. Man could say of it all the favorable things he chose, but nothing unfavorable. Reason might be free as long as it commended, as long as it flattered even, however extravagantly; but the same probity, the same impartiality, commended in the critic or the judge in other spheres, was immediately pronounced insufferable and impious. This very power we vaunted in face of the Church of Rome on the one hand, and fanatical Protestant sects on the other, we adjudged unworthy of a hearing, when it deprecated our own superstitions and errors: when it impeached our peculiar doctrines, it was immediately outlawed.

In vain the conviction was suppressed, that we were false to the great principle of the Reformation. What real difference was there between us and the Romanists? Did we not systematically avail ourselves of the immense influence of hereditary religion to crush reason with threats, with supplications, with appeals to the hopes and fears of men?

And how much more despicable were we? for, while adopting the method of the Mother Church, we condemned her for employing it. Where was the sincerity, the manliness, the virtue, of professing to be guided by reason and conscience, when, the moment they revolted from an unreasonable or immoral statement of theology or Scripture, they were pronounced utterly unreliable?

The conviction became settled, that candor and consistency were not encouraged by the spirit of Evangelicalism, but rather the practice of repeating the notions and theories of particular denominational leaders. It was safer to agree with Andrew Fuller or Robert Hall than with the whole college of the apostles, or with Jesus Christ, if they and the Christians of their day had misunderstood them. From time to time, facts came to me which were not so regarded by the denomination; and the number of them increased as I studied the Scriptures carefully. For example, Jesus Christ could not have regarded the Old Testament as infallible, even where it claims as much formally. He substitutes for the old law (Deut. xix. 21), "And thine eye shall not pity; but life shall go for life, eye for eye, tooth for tooth, hand for hand, foot for foot" (Matt. v. 39), "But I say unto you, that ye resist not evil; but whosoever shall smite thee on thy right cheek, turn to him the other also."

Yet in that very book of Deuteronomy (iv. 2)

it is written, "*Ye shall not add unto the word which I command you, neither shall ye diminish aught from it.*" Again, the standards of morality vary in the Scriptures. In the teaching of Christ, the love of enemies was enjoined; in the Old Testament, revenge was preached. Christ said, "Do good to them that hate you;" the Psalms commended the man who should murder the babes of Babylonian mothers (Ps. cxxxvii.); and against personal or political enemies prayers were breathed, that the greatest calamities might overtake them for their enmity; that they might die, become subject to a wicked genius, even to Satan; that their children might be beggars, spurned by every one; that they might fall victims to dishonest men, and be unfortunate in business (Ps. cix.). Further, Paul expected the Second Advent in his own lifetime. There could be no doubt of this, in view of his statement (1 Cor. xv. 51); and consequently he could have had no idea of establishing a universal Christian church. Then, there was the doctrine of the sabbath. I found it was not a Christian institution; that, in the whole of the New Testament such a fault as sabbath-breaking is not even mentioned; that the Lord's Day, like the Lord's Supper, was peculiar to

Christians, and distinct from ecclesiastical days. Further, I saw how arbitrarily Old Testament prophecies were applied in the New; the fallacious argument from the word "seed" in 1 Cor. xv. These were matters of fact among well-informed and impartial critics; but I dared not be understood to recite these in any representative Baptist assembly. I felt the strong hand of external authority tightening its grasp in proportion as I was preparing to resist it. There, in my own denomination, that I had loved, and boasted of as free, loyal to truth, enlightened, was a church authority which required as vulgar credulity as that implied in the Roman Church; viz., that a man can eat the human body of the Lord Jesus in masticating bread : for it insisted a living man was devoured by a fish, lived within it three days, and then was vomited, unharmed, upon the beach; that a man actually went up to the skies in a carriage of fire, drawn by horses of fire, not only uninjured, but in the sublimest condition of happiness; that the very material blood of Jesus had atoning and infinite value. The denomination was not prepared to discuss these questions, except with the foregone conclusion, that the received opinion was substantially true. Orthodoxy said, Write freely; but writing freely meant, as the term was used, tracing over already written characters. Still, what I knew thus far suggested only doubt and anxiety. It was destructive. The light pained; yet it was grateful. There was a keen sense of satisfaction in finding out error, like flinging away counterfeit coins when we have no better to replace them. These discoveries threw suspicion on the whole of religion. But was it my duty to proclaim them to the world? The possibility of losing place and name among beloved brethren was painful beyond words. Then the idea occurred of morbid sensitiveness. Was I magnifying trifles, over-concerned about minor things? Was I neglecting the duty of a navigator, in thinking of the barnacles of the ship? Now the resolution was half formed to speak with candor and caution the truth as it came, unmindful of consequences. The admission was insufferable, that a man could not tell the the truth in a Baptist church! Episcopalians, Presbyterians, Methodists, might shun the severe statement; but Baptists! — there at home in England they had groaned in dungeons and died at the stake for personal conviction. From earliest childhood, Baptist lips had said, "Tell the truth, though it ruin you." For ten years I had thanked God I belonged to a sect which could endure social ostracism, but could not turn a deaf ear to truth.

Such reflections made me deride myself for the moment; affection grew hysterical, and one was ready to blindly submit, and abjectly confess the revolt of reason as a guilty thing. Less amiable moods supervened. In presence of ignorant and prosperous affirmation, audacious and ostentatious sectarian conceit, a voice within derided. Emotion withered before the presence of superstition and error in the place of truth, though that place was my father's, and my religious home. That voice taunted in derision: "Yes, abandon truth. Settle down: be a humble, safe, useful man. Say what others say; do what others do. Indorse the unreasonable and the fanatical, that you may live in happiness, and be in death free from the brand of heretic. And then go to that God who is nothing if He be not holy, — the God of truth and righteousness."

Amid the conflict, I read on, thought on; avoided rash statements, needless divergences from accustomed and hereditary ideas and practices. God could not require me to assume the sorrows and burdens of a reformer, while as yet

I had not the reformer's grasp of newer forms of truth, nor his power of endurance.

It might be my society would sustain me, even if the denomination protested. But it was impossible to hold the truth without advancing; or to state it frankly, naturally, as we do contemporaneous events, without awakening apprehension and hostility. For authority, wherever it exists, is imperious, and demands unqualified submission. Facts, recognized as such by orthodoxy, could not be presented in a realistic way, without offence. For example: it is customary to say, Peter denied his Lord; but offensive to say, Peter grew most profane, and cursed, and swore he knew nothing of Jesus. It is proper to say, David had many wives and concubines, and fell into grievous sin; but highly improper to say, he was a very wicked man, — brutal, lustful, arrogant, — even though we speak with as deep an emphasis of his repentance, and continued struggle after a nobler life.

It is orthodox to say, Jesus was as much a man as though he had not been God; yet I dared not to speak of him as I would of a great and holy man. I might as well have smote him, with the soldiers (in the estimation of my old friends), as to say, Jesus renounced domestic ties, forewent the happiness of wife and child; because no real prophet would so encumber himself. He went on his mission alone; because he knew it might end in death! He would leave no widow to weep at his cross; no little children to clasp, in their dimpled hands, his bleeding feet, and cry, heart-broken, for their crucified father! As I dwelt on the tender pathos of such thoughts, I asked, Is the leaven of celibacy purged away from us? Why can such thoughts be derogatory to real manhood? If Christ actually was a man, why should wife and child degrade his memory more than mother and sister and brethren?

It became most evident, that men, generally speaking, are not themselves when they have to do with sacred things. The reasoning powers are enthralled by the fancy; the fancy is besotted by false teaching and ignorant fears. They are beside themselves with anxiety about their future fortune. Whatever they are in the ordinary walks of life, here they are weak, credulous, and childish. Truth is trampled down, unconsciously, in the scramble for heaven! Wherever men are unusually anxious about the destiny of their souls, it seems they are specially superstitious and unmindful of exactness in instruction. In proportion that undue reverence is felt for the letter of Scripture, I concluded, its spirit is obscured. There was the Bible prominent everywhere, upheld as a priceless treasure, preached from, quoted as the final authority, learned by heart; commentaries, great and small, on all hands; preachers who were specially educated to elucidate its meaning: yet I knew, as I know an oak from a fir tree, that the prevailing interpretations were *mainly* contrary to the original, the native, the obvious sense. The people of the churches, as a rule, appeared to me, after deliberate and anxious observation, to have no better idea of the Bible — of its continuous sense, of its arguments, of the meaning of its allegories and parables, of its underlying philosophical and theological doctrines — than the ordinary, superficial reader of general literature has of the historical outline, poetical beauty, and mythological coherency of Homer.

If it were placed in their hands divested of ecclesiastical glosses, Orientalism, and antique English phraseology; if the continuous sense were obvious; if the tender and poetical aroma of venerable associations which linger about words were dissipated, — almost every part would convey a different sense. If people really knew what was in the Bible, if they really knew how it came to be what it is to men, one is sure religion would seriously suffer for a time, great harm would be done to even the most reverent and truth-loving. Indeed, few men of any class can bear to be told all that the Bible really teaches: that it repeatedly and cordially approves of moderate indulgence in intoxicating drinks; that it indorses slavery, and favors monarchical institutions, as truly as it rebukes excess, cruelty, and tyranny. Henceforth, there was a chasm between me and my people. I must learn caution, must practise concealment, must endeavor not to say all I knew; or else disturb their peace, and wreck my own usefulness.

Careful exegesis, critical study of the Scriptures, only deepened and widened the gulf. What was the use of knowing more about the Bible, when such knowledge destroyed frankness and imposed constraint? And where would all this lead? If I persisted in finding out the truth, and found as startling discoveries further in the interior, what would the end be? was my own peace of mind safe? would the Bible be left? would Christ be left? would — God? Should I come at length to weep in despair, or jest in soulless frivolity, before the blank wall of

Secularism? Not devils, but angels, seemed to stand, with the drawn sword of menace, in the way to light and freedom. I wondered if I could be a virtuous man, and dare all consequences; knowing, too, I could not be, and consent to ignorance and dissimulation. The thought of John Locke came to me: "For he that examines, and, upon a fair examination, embraces an error for a truth, has done his duty more than he who embraces the profession (for the truths themselves he does not embrace) of the truth, without having examined whether it be true or no. . . . He that takes up the opinions of any church in the lump, without examining them, has truly neither searched after nor found truth; but has only found those that he thinks have found truth, and so receives what they say with implicit faith, and *so pays them the homage that is due only to God.*"

REVIEW OF CHURCH HISTORY.

"Church history has not yet been written as alone written it ought to be,—with truth, knowledge, and impartiality. Church history, falsely written, is a school of vain-glory, hatred, and uncharitableness; truly written, it is a discipline of humility, charity, of mutual love; written in a veracious and unsectarian spirit, every religious community is herein taught that it has cause enough to blush for its adherents."
—SIR WILLIAM HAMILTON.

CHAPTER III.

REVIEW OF CHURCH HISTORY.

I NEED not expatiate on the mental suffering experienced, the sense of the unreality of all things, which often pressed like an incubus. Suffice it to say, no language more accurately expresses the sorrows of many an hour than these words of F. Robertson's: "It is an awful moment, when the soul begins to find that the props on which it has blindly rested so long, are, many of them, rotten, and begins to suspect them all; when it begins to feel the nothingness of many of the traditionary opinions which have been received with implicit confidence, and, in that horrible insecurity, begins also to doubt whether there be any thing to believe at all. It is an awful hour — let him who has passed through it say how awful — when this life has lost its meaning, and seems shrivelled into a span; when the grave appears to be the end of all, human goodness nothing but a name, and the sky above this universe a dead expanse, black with the void from which God himself has disappeared!"

I resolved to be true to myself; to hold on, as the same prophet wrote, "to those things which are certain still,— the grand, simple landmarks of morality;" to do the best work I could, under the circumstances, and speak the truth as it came to me, come what might.

Determined, however, not to rest in doubt, but to read every thing which might throw light on the problems which distressed me, I had for some time read church history, Christian biography, the works of Robertson, Rowland, Williams, and Max Müller, Coleridge's prose works, Alger's "Doctrine of a Future Life," Channing, Dean Stanley, Greg; then, other works which alarmed and fascinated at the same moment. Matthew Arnold, with his portrait of Marcus Aurelius, put to shame the pious assurance with which I had been accustomed to consign all not-Christian saints to the limbo of moral degradation. Miss Cobbe, with her combined neology and rich devotion of spirit, taught me to hope that the soul might find rest in God, and come into the communion of Christ, when priests and priest-wrought literature were all waived away. And Rénan, while he vexed me with his jaunty air in treading holy ground, convinced me of the utter shallowness and one-sidedness of the Biblical criticism of Evangelicals.

Buckle, Lecky, and Sir William Hamilton were valuable; neutralizing the partiality of ecclesiastical historians and philosophers. For it seemed to me, from Neander to Stanley, the fairest writers were too courtier-like in their treatment of disparaging facts in sacred history, too much in the habit of using euphemisms and apologetic phrases, for a plain man to realize the true character of what they were describing. Indeed, one was tempted to think, that if such golden pens would do for the Newgate calendar what they have done for the priests, posterity therefrom would have difficulty in believing its personages were abject or incorrigible criminals.

The effect of extended acquaintance with history, especially church history, was twofold. As the past rose before me, — coming near to the peoples of all religions; looking into the face of good men of all creeds and races; thinking of Zoroaster, of Socrates, of Plato, of Gautama, of Confucius, of Mohammed, of Augustine, of Arius, of Saint Bernard, of Xavier, of Pascal, of Arndt, of Luther, of Servetus, of Erasmus, of Jeremy Taylor, of Gibbon, of Hume, of Chillingworth, of Raleigh, of Cudworth, of Lindsay, of Coleridge, — as I looked across Christendom; breathed the very air of the presence of the Newmans, Alford, Bunsen, Arnold, Martineau, Kalisch, Prof. Jowett, Stanley, and all their ilk, — I said, "Gather my soul with the saints," though it exile me from my fathers and brethren. Let Calvin have his own! these are God's own, — his own by right of their moral majesty, their piety, their heroic service of mankind, whatever the complexion of their creed. As the multitudes of fanatics of every age passed in review, — Donatists, crusaders, ephemeral sects, revivalists, — down to our time, I discerned, beneath appearances, the deep, earnest, restless striving of the ignorant, the duped, the terrified, after peace, righteousness, and truth; all seeking, however ignorantly, after God. I saw them going thither, — some with wild gesticulations, bleeding feet, bandaged eyes; some clinging to the arm or skirts of others; some shouting "Eureka!" and rejoicing in delusion: but the most I saw limped or crawled. For priests, presbyters, preachers, all well-meaning as the Chinese mother, had from the first deformed their feet; had pressed and bandaged and unshaped them, by forcing reason into their respective sectarian theological creeds. I saw, too, the millions of orderly and prosaic worshippers, from week to week, quietly doing their duty, unstirred by genius, and usually unalarmed by the dragon of priestcraft, which lies quiet when unirritated and well fed.

In contemplation of the holy catholic church of God's children, mad or sane, frenzied or at peace,—all these, who were clinging, however blindly or fearfully, to moral good,—I felt I had no quarrel with it: indeed, in that hour, I came into conscious inheritance of the goodly fellowship of the redeemed of every country and people and kindred and tongue. Toward the untheologic masses of my own communion, a truer, because less partial, sympathy was inspired. I saw they need not be as a son forced to endure for a season the sight of the strange indulgence of the Father toward a proscribed and ruined brother; but as those who feel that the Infinite Heart, while it blesses those of every faith, says to each of them, "Son, thou, too, art ever with me, and all that I have is also thine." And when I left them, it was as one who might have left the side of the elder brother, not because I loved him less, but because I loved the Father and his household more.

But the history of doctrines, of clerical theologians, of the perfunctionary manipulators of the religious sentiment and ecclesiastical interests, of persecutions, of controversies, of propagandism, — those things, which are so often regarded as Christianity, awakened nought but shame and scorn. To the simple foundation truths of Christianity, they seemed what the painted, fantastically adorned, and decaying mummy is to the living seed sometimes enclosed in its dead hand.

If the history of Christianity means the legitimate development of the teaching of Jesus, and the rise and progress of his spirit in the earth, it is not yet written. We have the history of the church, not of that kingdom of heaven Christ sought to establish more firmly among men. We have the story of the apostles, — of organized religion, — but not of the little children who are in the midst, like unto whom the most gifted and exalted must become ere they can enter this kingdom of natural godliness. While the student of ecclesiastical history must, if he be impartial and Christian, recognize in every age and station instances of the deepest piety and holiest zeal; while he must see the church has been oftentimes a power for good, — yet it is impossible, viewing it as a whole, speaking in general terms of its spirit and influence, to give any verdict save one of condemnation. The track of Juggernaut was never more deeply stained with blood. Clerical Christianity might be represented by the allegorical figure of War, with sword and torch in its hands, while Hate, Death, and Ruin are behind; its feet planted on the necks of Knowledge and Freedom. If, indeed, its record could be the record of one man ; if its virtues and crimes could be balanced ; if judgment could be passed by a fit tribunal, as on a solitary prisoner at the bar, — what voice in heaven or earth would be raised to stay its doom? And, when its course has been most pacific, what a spectacle of humiliation is it to those animated with Christ's spirit! From its most august conventions to the meetings of modern convocations, from ecumenical councils to sectarian conferences, despite the learning and the piety which have never been taken from her, — how redolent of puerility, semi-statement, evasion, superstition, intimidation, passion, favoritism, equivocation, party-spirit, shuffling, boasting, hypocrisy, and uncharitableness are they all! The evil spirit of sacerdotalism has ever been dominant.

Founded by prophets, the church has been captured and guided by priests. Nothing impressed me more than the conflict of these elements. I saw that these two classes existed side by side. The shame of the church came from the one; its glory, from the other. There were priests among the self-styled prophets, and prophets among the priests. Every minister of religion, Papal or Protestant, approximates to the character of one or the other. Some are *now* priest, and *then* prophet; the one at the altar, and the other by the fireside. The priest is ever narrowly educated, ignorant however learned, sanctimonious, time-serving, unfair, fond of power; so adroit in reflecting the average sentiment of those by whom his interests are served; so plausible in his representations of the discreditable in the church, or the absurd in its doctrine; so skilful in the appliance of terror and advantage, — that the people, even the strong-minded, shrink from admitting to themselves, what is only too evident, viz., his shallowness, his selfishness, his vanity, his specious casuistry, his tendency to chicane, his effeminacy, his bigotry. The prophets are the men alive to what is true, though it be unprofitable and anathematized; to what is false, though it be ancient, popular, and in the place of infallible dogma: ever on the side of the good, even when they are crucified and scorned; ever against the bad, even when they are rich, exalted, and reputedly pious. The prophets ever exalt reason, virtue, truth. With sublime self-abandonment, they cry, "We will be on the side of God, though God be not on ours:" like him, the chiefest of them all, who dared to die for the truth, even when the God of truth seemed so to withdraw Himself from the dying eyes of His servant, that the heroic sufferer, in the article of death, cried "Why hast Thou forsaken me?" The prophet is content to speak the truth, and leave it with men, not over-careful to conciliate, or to ask what advantage shall arise to him therefrom. Yes: evermore, in all religions, these two struggle; the prophet ever having the worst of it. The prophet announces the truth; the priest slays him, and makes, long after, profit by his words. The prophet perishes in dungeon or desert: yet the day comes when his bones are gathered up, and lie upon the altar, amid the sacred relics; but the bones of the priest seldom mingle with them.

In reading church history, I came to the following conclusion:—

The Baptists were and are, essentially, a variety of Latin Christianity, in the same sense the Latin Church is a variety of ecclesiastical religion. They stand to it in the same relation, it stands to the more ancient faiths of the world. The Latin Church is Christ, *plus* Judaism, Oriental philosophies, and pagan ecclesiasticisms. The Puritan, and with it the Baptist Church, is the Latin Church, *minus* the coarser developments of doctrine, the splendors of ritual, hierarchical dignity and power, and the historic imagination. Its distinctive tenets and peculiar spirit had, for ages, clung to the Mother Church, on the one side, as ultramontanism (as we now call it) had, on the other. The Donatists were their ecclesiastical ancestors. Erigena, Berengar, and other great Romanist theologians, said, in the dialect of the scholar and with the caution of the priest, what was afterward in a popular form disseminated among the common people as Protestant doctrine.[1] Every thing it had came through the channel of Romanism. It had no means of knowing any thing whatever of Christianity or of religious dogma, save as it was learned from the Roman Church. The whole Puritan movement was not, and could not, have

---

[1] "Latin Christianity," vol. iii. bk. vi. ch. ii.

been a return to the religion of Jesus and the apostles, but a reformation of Catholicism: for they had no means of knowing what the former was; but they knew, to a great extent, what Romanism ought to be.

If *they* had succeeded in regiving the religion of Jesus, it had been as great a proof of divine inspiration as the regiving of truth by Jesus. Impartial history was unknown. They were shut up to the literature of the church. Primitive ideas of doctrine and practice survived only among existing corruptions and misrepresentations. The Bible was not only the Catholic version, but bore its interpretation.

The Reformers imagined the sacred writings lay before them substantially as they were in the apostolic church. They regarded the epistles of Peter as Paul was supposed to have done, or Paul's as Peter was supposed to have regarded them. They had no idea that these apostolic writers controverted each other's opinions, and that the proof lies in their extant speeches and writings. The arguments of sacred writers were not to them ratiocinative methods of . demonstrating truth, but a mere fashion by which divine revelations were uttered. It was never asked, Is the point proven? for every line of the argument was considered above proof. Nor is this denied by well-informed and candid Baptists. In the work frequently quoted in these pages, by Mr. Aldis, on "Christian Union," it is said of the Puritan Reformers, and consequently of Baptist:—

"The Reformers had, indeed, the written word to appeal to, by which all confessed themselves equally bound; but that word required to be interpreted, and the given interpretation was the law. Every believer, however, claimed the right of interpretation; while the aids of it were few, and the difficulties many. The path they trod was new. There had been no translations of the Scriptures into the languages of the common people. Copies of the original were rare, and competent scholarship in them rarer still. The most learned men had fewer helps in Biblical criticism than are now accessible to the teachers in our sabbath-schools. To a certain extent they had been acquainted with the words of the New Testament. Ecclesiastical terms had been stereotyped in the Church of Rome; but false meanings had been attached to them. Men could look at no theological subject but through these false media. They had much to unlearn; to strip off false disguises; to rise superior to the latent influence of centuries."

Whatever was essential to the Christian life and character, whatever was necessary to salvation, they had found *as* Romanists, or acknowledged their Puritan leaders had. They did not start anew, as Mr. Aldis affirms: "*All assumed they were Christians before they were Protestants.* Neither Luther nor Calvin thought himself unconverted while in the Romish Church, nor, consequently, that all of it was anti-Christ. It was, therefore, a question of degree in the negation of Romanism." Protestants have not ceased to be protestant: all are protesting Roman Catholics. The Baptist protests against Anglicanism; Anglicanism protests against Romanism; and Protestantism means nothing, if it does not mean, feeling itself to be Christian after the type of the Mother Church; bound to her by bonds it either will not, or cannot, sever, it conserves its sense of duty by protesting, and defends its prolonged schismatic attitude by reference to her indifference to.its protest. The United States were, immediately before the Revolutionary War, a politically protestant people, still a colony of England. To-day they cease to be politically protestant, because they have severed their relations with the parent country, and adopted a new *régime;* and her opinions, doctrines, laws, policies, customs, and authority are no more to them than to any other independent nation. But as long as it was a colony it was its duty to be loyal; and, when its heart was alienated, it as much proclaimed its loyalty as its wrongs by protest; and protest only ceased when revolution began. The church was not revolutionized, — it simply gave birth to children called reformers; but none the less children because alienated, and not the less children because the mother shunned and they protested.

The differences of doctrine and ritual is the difference of the vegetation of temperate and tropical zones. There is the same species in both; but a fuller, ranker, more imposing growth in the one. The doctrine of the Trinity is as unintelligible and as much insisted on. Their Christologies are equally superstitious and idolatrous. True, they draw the magic circle round one sacred figure, and call it God; and forbid Mary, the mother, to be called the mother of God, but as inconsistently as The Church forbade the grandmother, Anne, to be called the grandmother of God. The ideas of sacrificial atonement, of interventionary prayer, of plenary inspiration, of the meritoriousness of solemnity and discomfort are common to both. Their eschatology was identical, with the exception of purgatory. Their hagiographa was purged of all saints from a certain date; but the Romish conception of patriarchs, prophets, and apostles, and of all personages mentioned in Scripture, remained. They asserted the right of private judgment, as ignorant of its nature and requirements as they were of the origin and authentic sense of the Scriptures. The Protestant idea of private judgment in matters of religious opinion was but a more extensive application of a right never challenged by the ancient church. It had always recognized the right of individuals to choose opinions within certain limits. It denied the right within the sacred enclosure of truths which were positively defined and formulated as the teachings of the Divine Spirit.

The Reformers, with inadequate scholarship and undisguised prejudices, assumed to say what things should remain in that enclosure. In the excitement of strife and suffering, in a very whirlwind of feeling and indignation, they passed judgment on the relative worth and scripturalness of the individual doctrines of a system built up by ages of speculation and controversy ; and, while they were themselves divided, they drew a smaller circle around this pruned or mutilated system, and forbade Free Inquiry and Individualism ever to enter there. The old gods, divested of their finery, and selected from the crowds of inferior or more repulsive divinities, were transferred from the splendors of the old Pantheon to the white-washed walls of Puritanism, whose doors were guarded as vigilantly against Reason, and the devotion of whose worshippers was as intense and unquestioning.

"The very men who had headed the enthusiastic forces of the Reformation, as they broke down the old barriers of authority, and spread themselves, as springs of religious revolution, throughout Europe, are found, ere long, busy in collecting, consolidating, and placing anew under authority the spiritual energies which they had everywhere called forth. . . . So it came to pass that in the second stage of the Reformation the principle of authority had almost entirely superseded the principle of inquiry." [1]

The right of private judgment was ceded but for a moment. It was used as a war measure. Luther, Calvin, and all Evangelical Reformers employed it only for the purpose of their own emancipation from the church. They turned

[1] Principal Tulloch, in "Rational Theology in England in the Seventeenth Century."

their guns on their ecclesiastical mother; won their victory; then sought to spike them for ever, lest their own children might be tempted to contradict the filial instinct. Baptists had individually asserted the right in the face of Rome; congregationally, they asserted it in face of the Reformers with whom they had departed from the ancient communion. Yet even they retain the obliquity of vision which perceives nothing absurd in maintaining mutually destructive principles; so that, in regard to all who differ from their most cherished theological and ritualistic teachings, they are as intolerant as the papacy. Strange as it seems to them (and it is no stranger than a similar accusation brought by Protestants against Romanism), Baptists have no more liberty of reason and conscience, and respect their rights in others no more, than the Papal Church. The themes of discussion and the *causus belli* of controversy are different; but intolerance is as intolerant, and expulsion as inevitable, for all who assert unorthodox opinions. True, they vaunt the rights of conscience, and educated their members in the belief they are nowhere so affectionately cherished; but it is indisputable, that if any man have another or a wiser theory of the Divine nature than the Trinitarian, or of the efficacy of self-sacrificing philanthropy than the Augustinian, he *must* either keep it to himself, be disfellowshipped, or disfellowship himself. Does Rome do otherwise? Any man can believe what he likes, if he be silent, in spite of all the priests, or if he confesses his doubts to them and is silent to all others (for the loyal heretic, unfaithful to light and duty, is pitied as "the victim of Satanic temptation," or as the subject of occasional difficulties); and, if he speaks out, nothing worse than expulsion in some form overtakes him. The Seventh-Day Baptists, the Freewill Baptists, and the Disciples, were no doubt honest in their judgment; but fidelity to it cost them their place in the Baptist Church. It is a mockery of language to say this right is respected, while the real meaning is, " Judge as you will; but you must agree with us, or suffer." In point of fact, I saw in my denomination a pale print from the negative plates of Rome. We, too, had our Fathers : they were the Reformers and deceased theologians. Our papacy : in an oligarchical form, living eminent divines. Our creeds : denominational literature. Our church consciousness : Baptist usage. Our "Index Expurgatorius :" the religious press. Rome asks no more than that men shall judge in her favor: so Baptists have all their judgments anticipated. The Roman Church excommunicates Père Hyacinthe; the Baptists tell Alexander Campbell, "We regret your conclusions differ from ours. We stand here facing each other; but we must part. Which shall make the distance between us? We prefer you should do it." And, if my former co-religionists point to the attendant sufferings of excommunicated and reforming Romanists, I ask them, Are their tender mercies less cruel? Is it nothing to be separated by a gulf deep as the grave from all the traditions, interests, and friends of one's childhood, youth, and early ministry, because one cannot agree with their opinions? They do not, indeed, consciously persecute; for, whatever their creed, they are Christians of a humane type: nevertheless, they do cause men to suffer for opinion's sake; they do brand men as heretics; they do cast them out from all that was revered and cherished, and waive them away to God's uncovenanted mercies. The difference between mother and daughter is in degree, not in kind. Rome conscientiously persecutes: it persecutes by rule, with circumstance, with severity. The Baptists are kinder, their method less systematic, their procedure less imposing, their anger more moderate; but their excommunication is as real. But the Romanists are more consistent: they have a coherent theological system, defined dogmas, and codified laws; their adherents are taught from the first the conditions of fellowship are passive obedience and subscription. The Baptists, on the other hand, placed the Bible before me, and said, "This, as God gave it, is the only authority in faith and practice. Agree with it, and you have done all we require." That book is in my hand. I believe, I revere, I hold fast its teachings; honestly try to obey its laws, and live in the light of its examples, and can conclude no other than as I have concluded. Reason and conscience have been my teachers. I have studied in the spirit of Christ, as I imagine, and now am assured God approves the verdict reason and conscience give. With a humble but resolute purpose to live out that same spiritual life, so long fostered by my old co-religionists, I must go away, or be cast away; while the most ignorant affirmer of denominational crudities is allowed to remain unchallenged, and to rank as one true to "the faith as once delivered to the saints."

The remarks here made with regard to the

early Baptists should not be understood as exhaustive of my opinion of them. The purpose of this narrative hardly admits of the eulogies it would be otherwise fitting to lavish on their courage, their conscientiousness, their piety, and the services they rendered to the cause of religious liberty. What they did they thought was radical, consistent, and final. The Puritan name must ever be held in honor. But can as much be said of the spirit of modern Protestantism? Have denominations, as such, advanced one-half the distance in two hundred years that the early Puritans and Baptists did in fifty? Have they, in our day, testified as much for liberty of thought as the prelate Jeremy Taylor said in his "Liberty of Prophesying" for their crushed and simple-minded founders? Have they advanced one step in Biblical criticism and speculative theology beyond Bunyan? Do they welcome new opinions or original statements on far more important subjects, as cordially as the godly and despised citizens of London welcomed the new theories of Mr. John Spilsbury, or Mr. William Kiffin, as to the nature of baptism? With nothing but texts from a book obscured by false interpretations, whose meaning they believed they had made out, they assailed the orthodox theory on that subject; and so impressed were they with the sense of truth's imperious demand for utterance, that, to be conscientious on so inconsiderable a subject, they separated themselves from their churches. Yet to-day, in the light of the frankest and fullest Biblical criticism; with more aids for the understanding of Scripture than any period before, — in an age rejuvenescent with the spirit of tolerance and progress, — my friends stand with so antiquated a religious vocabulary that it is unintelligible or humorous outside of Evangelicalism. With so effete a theological system, that it is doomed to carry on its work among masses animated by the theological spirit, while devoid of the theological sense: masses *the better part* of whom minimize the mischievousness of its crude opinions and superstitions by a practical good sense, which fastens on rational ideas and active beneficence, in utter disregard of consistency; *the mediocre part*, of the good-hearted, making much of their creed, attributing every spiritual blessing to its influence, albeit speculative theology, good or bad, cannot penetrate them, nor superstitions of any hue affect the complexion of their lives; while *the third part*, the egotistic and ill-natured, make the theology of the sect the pretext for the gratification of the pride, bigotry, vanity, self-assertion, and interference in the affairs of others, which propensities would vent themselves about other subjects, if not about this. May the day soon come when the more liberal, the more enlightened, the more rationalistic and courageous individuals who dissent within the ranks may so assert themselves, that the denomination shall awake from its long sleep, and take from the altar the seeds, — the principles it has so long revered, — and sow them; insisting, with the vanguard of the Church of the Future, what its Fathers said with a narrower meaning, but with as catholic a spirit: *Truth is sacred by itself and for itself alone! Righteousness is the only bond of perfectness, and the only test of opinion. Absolute religious freedom is the right of every man, concerning every theme or practice.* And should I live to see that day, Baptists will not be surprised that I said, "I am a Unitarian because I was a Baptist."

Now I endeavored to trace the origin of that Latin or Roman Catholic Christianity, of which the Baptists and all the other Western sects are offshoots. Whence came these dogmas, such as the trinity of persons in the Godhead, the Deity of Jesus, and the personality of the Holy Spirit?

How came it to pass that the pure and simple teaching of the Lord was supplanted by the artificial doctrines which are now called the Gospel? I found there were decisive moments in the history of the church when controversialists forced their subtle speculations into the place of divine truth. One of these epochs was in the fourth century. Before that time, Christianity presented a completely different aspect, and was imbued by a different spirit. Pre-Nicene Christianity was essentially Greek: its spirit, its theologies, its literature, its bishops, its churches, were all Grecian. The opinions which afterward became the creed of orthodoxy in the Western Church were then the speculations of an Oriental sect. Before the Nicene council, we find an era of violent discussion. The men engaged in it gave no greater evidence of the special inspiration of the Holy Ghost than congressmen wrangling over a party question. One says this after a long pause. It is a terrible assertion to make; but let any man acquaint himself with the history of that period, and it is impossible for him to arrive at any other conclusion. Indeed, Mr. Aldis says, "The very ministers of the Gospel were thus enfeebled and corrupted. They became obsequious hirelings or spiritual tyrants. Some were sycophants, the slaves of meanness and pride; and others were the victims of covetousness or ambition, fired with the lust of distinction or gain. Some were men of strong imagination and slender judgment, largely imbued with the Gentile superstition, and but little acquainted with the spirituality of the Gospel; and they first defended as lawful, and next urged as useful, and at last enforced as essential, a whole circle of carnal rites, which repulsed the spirit of truth, and eclipsed the cross of Christ. Others, being men of subtle minds, and enamoured of the Platonic philosophy, were not satisfied with 'the foolishness of preaching,' 'nor with the simplicity of Christ.' They tried to render the Gospel more attractive by elaborating and embellishing its dogmas. They refined on what was simple, and perplexed what was clear, by introducing a host of doctrines, which few could understand, and none determine." [1]

It was by such men the whole character of Christ's religion was changed,— so subtly and successfully changed, that Christendom to-day, in her most Protestant sects, knows not the fatal perversion which was effected. Metaphy-

[1] "Excellent Glory."

sicians and priests jostled, and then ousted, the simple, natural followers of Christ. The Polemicists distracted the attention of Christians from spiritual growth and practical virtue to "doctrines which few could understand, and none could determine;" and, from that day to this, their forms have cast the deepest shadow in the house of God. The nearer we approach the Nicene council, the more violent do these dissensions become. The element which gave power to the Roman Church was a schismatic party of primitive Christianity; and Rome is in reality the oldest and greatest of heretics. I had often felt there might be some force in the theory of a dynamic process of development in doctrine,— that the Divine Spirit may have so revealed truth from age to age, by means of the official church, that, after all, it might be our duty to accept post-apostolic statements with even more consideration than those of the sacred writers. I conceived of the Roman Church under Pascal's figure,— as one man always learning, always extracting the essence of truth in heresies and speculations, and storing it in formulated creeds and confessions. But this man of a thousand years, this august, authoritative, self-important person, stood in a moment, as I looked on him from before the Nicene council, *a heretic* himself, cursed and spurned by an older and more venerable man, who had received the Gospel from the lips of the apostles themselves, — a heretic, cursed and spurned by that same Greek Church, corrupted though it be, to the present day. Here, then, I exclaimed, are two church conciousnesses. Who can decide between them? Why need we try? For the Greek Church is not surer of the procession of the Spirit from the Father only, than it is of the heretical character of the Latin Church; and the Latin Church is not surer of the procession of the Spirit from both the Father and the Son, than it is of the schismatic nature of the Eastern communion. Church consciousness curses church consciousness! who shall bless?

As I saw the kind of men who established Trinitarianism, as the circumstances under which the most conspicuous creed of Christendom was planted were reviewed, the idea of special divine guidance became utterly untenable.

As Dean Milman says, a general council is "a battle field in which a long train of animosities and hostilities is to come to an issue. Men, therefore, meet with all the excitement, the estrangement, the jealousy and antipathy, engendered by a fierce and obstinate controversy. They meet to triumph over their adversaries, rather than dispassionately to investigate truth. Each is committed to his opinions, each exasperated by opposition, each supported by a host of intractable followers." [1] It was under such conditions that a sectarian theory, a party notion, about the nature of God was elevated from the obscurity of individual opinion to the rank of an all-important dogma of the church. It was decided by numbers, by craft, by intimidation. As I witnessed, so to speak, the Nicene council, reading Stanley's "Eastern Church" and Hefele's History, remembering the tremendous issues which have resulted therefrom, I was ready to question my own sanity. Could such a colossal structure as the belief of ages really rest upon such foundations as these? There, as its president, was the unbaptized semi-pagan, yet august Emperor Constantine, destined to be baptized on his deathbed by Arian hands, when spurned from the altar of the sun by its indignant flamens. • Here was Cæsar exalted to the chief place in the church, not for his piety, not for his theological ability, but for his rank and

"Latin Christianity," i. 156.

station: on his right hand, and on his left, were angry men, who indulge in recriminations, accusations, and even *blows*. The language used would disgrace the lowest demagogue. Athanasius himself spoke of Arians as devils, maniacs, dogs, wolves, lions, hydras, eels, cuttle-fish, beetles, leeches, swine. Here are men who must vote according to the dictates of one or other of the great leaders, or lose their position and homes. As Dr. Jortin, quoted by Stanley, says, they were influenced "by the dread of passing for heretics, and of being calumniated, reviled, hated, anathematized, excommunicated, imprisoned, banished, fined, beggared, starved, if they refused to submit; by the love of peace and quiet; by the hatred of contention; by compliance with an active body and imperious spirit; by a deference to the majority; by a love of dictating and domineering, of applause and respect; by vanity and ambition; by a total ignorance of the question in debate, or a total indifference about it; by private friendships; by enmity and resentment; by old prejudices; by hopes of gain; by an indolent disposition; by good nature and the fatigue of attending; by the desire to be at home," &c. Such were the motives which secured the greatest step toward the establishment of the Trinitarian creed, and determined for fifteen hundred years the orthodoxy of Western Christendom. To say these were the only motives, would be unjust; but we may and must conclude that the majority was secured by means of them, and that majority really fixed the kind of belief which should prevail. And this assembly is but a type of all councils, of whatever age or church. Personal, partisan, and political influences are as dominant as in any secular, deliberative body. The majority is accounted authoritative: the still small voice of wisdom is drowned in the multitudinous vociferations of mediocrity, partisanship, sectarianism, ignorance, bigotry, and craft. It has been said, "Majorities are never right." Be that as it may, such majorities as have fixed the creed of Christendom should not weigh with us a moment. Ecclesiastical theology had evidently no higher source than party legislation. Gladly would I have joined my co-religionists in affirming that our doctrines were immediate growths from the Bible, and that their history could be disentangled from that of the Roman Church; but this were absurd. Orthodoxy, whether at Rome or Geneva, in the Mother Church or in the sects, is as much connected with the theology established at that council as twigs are with the roots and trunk of the tree to which they belong. But for the council of the church, but for majorities gained by such motives as swayed the Nicene assembly, it is clear no such doctrine as the Deity of Jesus would have come down to us. At least, it is clear to me, that, were it credible that the Holy Ghost inspired any of its great decisions, I could as easily believe all were inspired in the same way; for I must hold to the dogma which every council presupposed, viz., the infallibility of the church. The dogma of transubstantiation rests on the same authority as that of the Deity of Jesus. Both are as irrational, the one as the other. If we are to reject one thing contrary to reason, we must all. If reason ever brings herself to say, I have no right to reject this dogma, which appears to me unreasonable, then she abdicates her functions for ever, or incurs the shame of inconsistency. For me there is no middle course: I must be where I am, or else submit wholly, blindly, humbly, to the great historic church of Eastern Christendom; I must ignore the past, I must ignore the Bible, I must ignore Latin Christianity, and say the Greek Church claims to have met from time to time, guided, inspired, by the Spirit of God. Under that guidance, she asserts alike her own infallibility in matters of faith, and the only true doctrine of God, of Christ, and of the eucharist. She also declares the schismatic nature of all who have separated from her. If the divinity of Jesus is true, then there is no room to question any thing she affirms. If there inheres in primitive organized Christianity the power of saying certain things which are contrary to reason and historic facts are truths, we can never discriminate between such dogmas. All are alike above reason; and yet it is only by reason we can discriminate. In other words, Protestantism, in all her sects, is an anomaly. There is not one church or clergyman who, if they were consistent, would remain an hour without submission to the Papal or Greek Church. Either they have no right to their theology, or they have no right to their Protestantism. There is no place for them: they are neither with nor against the church. Like the children of Israel, they have borrowed from the Egyptians, returning not again. They have blasphemed the source of the dogma on which their eternal hopes are built. They call Christ God, yet anathematize the church through whom alone the dogma was given. But to me the official church is without authority. I reject its claims wholly. Doing as I was bidden, yet more, while rejecting the claims of the ancient church, I reject, too, the claims of schismatic churches. But let me add, in rejecting the idea of the authority of the church or of churches, it is not meant to imply that divine truth is wholly revealed to the individual. There is a sacred dynamic consciousness; truth has been revealed from age to age; we are heirs of the wisdom of our forerunners. Very much of this revelation is stored in the Bible: what is here denied is, that this revelation has come through the clerical channel; that is, through the long succession of controversial divines. Church history is not the record of the church, any more than party politics is the record of a nation. It is the record of officials, and of the conflict of opinions, mainly among themselves. Religious people were enlisted on opposite sides, just as patriotic men were often found fiercely fighting in the cause of personal royal quarrels. They did not express their own views, but gave vent to their passions and prejudices. Insight into truth, is at an end when controversy begins; Truth dies by the sword drawn in her behalf;

people cease to reflect when they plunge into conflict. One no more cares to know what controversialists say in councils or assemblies, than one cares to know what a man says in delirium, or in the height of passion. The men who see the truth are men of reflection; the time to state it is when all is calm. If we want to know the truth about the political condition of the United States, we should not ask the demagogue in the midst of a campaign; or, if we knew and wished to state its true condition, that were not the time to speak. As Rowland Williams says, "You pronounce as an axiom that 'truth is best elicited by the conflict of opinions;' whereas, I hold that the truths which concern us most are brought home to us best by influences of an affectionate, social, or spiritual kind."

The men are hardly heard from who thought in patience and quietude, who cared not for the honors of place and power. We hear in the main from the men who had an interest — a personal interest — in speaking as they spoke. If there had been no Alexander nor Athanasius to vanquish Arius, no party to honor and applaud these combatants, we might never have heard of the Nicene controversy.

We turn from the study of such histories, saying, in the words attributed to Thomas à Kempis, "Happy is he whom truth teaches not by figures and words that pass away, but by an immediate communication of itself." "O God the truth, make me one with thee in everlasting love! I am weary of reading and hearing many things: in thee is all that I desire. Let all creatures be silent in thy sight: speak thou alone to me."

I now sought to trace the connection of ante-Nicene Christianity with that of the apostles; principally with the view of finding out the legitimacy of the claim that the New Testament books constituted, together with the Old, a sacred canon, — whether there was any thing in their origin, or in the indorsement of the sub-apostolic church, to warrant us in regarding these writings as sacred, apart from their intrinsic worth; *i.e.*, the truth we can see they contain. Others may be able to penetrate into the thick darkness of the period from which the alleged canon emerged; but I cannot. We know how the Christian doctrine of the Trinity arose, we know the men who called it into being; but who the persons were, what their piety, their wisdom, or their ability, who combined to fix the rank, the general sense, and relative authority of the early Christian writings, we do not know. The few early writers about whom any thing is known, were, on the authority of Westcott,[1] uncritical, in no way specially distinguished by sagacity and research, more or less credulous, uninformed as their Pagan contemporaries.

Think of the Revision Committee, — what a trifling task is theirs compared with that of fixing the sacred canon for all time! Yet who to-day would for a moment entertain the proposal of a new version of these Scriptures from unknown hands? Who would consent to receive, as an infallible rule, a selection from early writings made to-day by the most pious, learned, and trustworthy men?

The church idea and the canon must stand or fall together. We must grant to the Romanist (in the words of Rowland Williams), "that the church was before the Bible, as a speaker is before the voice; and that Holy Scripture is not the foundation of the Christian faith so much as its creature, its expression, its embodiment." Or else we must hold that these writings are the utterance of individuals to individuals; that their juxtaposition is providential; and that their

[1] "The Canon of New Testament," p. 8, 4th edition.

force, their authority, their eminence, is wholly due to the obvious truth within them. In other words, the question shaped itself to me, *Is Scripture privileged literature,* — is it among books what priests are among men? Is it of such a nature that we must receive it as orthodoxy requires, — as an organic whole, having uniformity of teaching, freedom from grave errors, and unbroken, unvarying authority? Or should we regard it as containing the word of God in remarkable fulness, as the brightest light which has shone on the pathway of the human race, as containing the sum of the religious inspirations of an eminently gifted and thoughtful people, as the most illustrious series of instances of historic truthfulness and simplicity? The conventional notion involves the mind in hopeless confusion and perplexity. Biblical critics have proven, beyond doubt, that the sacred writers fall into errors of fact; contradicting one another and ascertained historical data:[1]* that there could be

[1] Errata of the New Testament (Ed. Scherer), in "Progress of Religious Thought in France." Dr. Beard.

* This is not denied by intelligent Baptists. It is a curious fact that orthodox ingenuity has deduced from it an argument for the divine origin of the Bible. "The existence of difficulties in the Bible ought to create no surprise, if it be the book of God; since there are difficulties in all His works. This does but place the Bible on a level with the works of

no question as to the older books of the Jewish canon being a compilation from traditional sources; in all probability edited as late as the time of Ezra: that the Gospels are reminiscences of disciples of Jesus, written either by the evangelists or their successors, having all the imperfections of records written long after the conversations and events narrated from oral utterance: that the Epistles are of the nature of letters of a religious teacher and organizer to his disciples, containing advice, arguments, information, as all such letters do: and that the Apocalypse is the semi-political apostrophe of one of the early Christians to the proud and cruel oppressors of the primitive church. To reconcile these facts with the ecclesiastical theories of inspiration seemed to me not only futile, but impious. For, if the Bible contains the divine word, — the *ideas* which are able to make us wise unto salvation, — what valid excuse can we make for ourselves to God, if we have wasted time

---

nature, — the stones, the trees, the stars. Were it wholly free from difficulty, the presumption against its divine origin would certainly be more strong." In reply to objections that it does not "agree with facts, as in geology; because its doctrines are contrary to reason, as in the Trinity; and because its morals are impure, as in some Old Testament narratives." — *J. H. Hinton*, vol. vii. p. 401.

and talents in the endeavor so to represent the temple that we may swear by it, instead of devoting these energies and opportunities to His word and service? We have this treasure in earthen vessels; yet our orthodox brethren, unconsciously, distract attention from it, — indeed, awaken aversion, — by the attempt to prove the earthen vessel is of as pure gold as its contents. But it was urged, that the writers claim all that is claimed for them; and, if their testimony as to their own authority can be rejected, their writings are valueless.

In the first place, I found they never made any such claim. The often-quoted and most conspicuous proof-text in 2 Tim. iii. 16, had been seriously perverted: instead of teaching that the canonical writings of the Jew, his own epistles, and the, as yet, unwritten portions of the New Testament, were alone the inspired books, he taught, that "all Scripture given by inspiration of God was profitable."

In the next place, I grew convinced, that if they had, they *ought* not, — no man *ought*, — to make such a claim; and no man ought to believe him, if he did; and no man *could*, until antiquity and ecclesiasticism had exalted his literary effort into the hazy and delusive atmosphere of canonicity.

For, to admit this claim would be to admit that the prerogative inheres in some individuals of asserting that any thing they are themselves convinced is a message from the Deity is binding on the minds and hearts of mankind to the end of time. The church could adopt the writings of Joseph Smith, and force them on men, by the very theory they hold of the inspiration of the sacred writers. All that is necessary is to assume he had the right to claim infallible inspiration, the right to say, "What I have written was revealed to me by God as the canon of religious life and belief." Then, it is evident men must harmonize what they think is truth with what he says is truth; his words must be made to mean a great deal he never intended ; errors must be all explained away; discrepancies, harmonized ; immoral opinions, palliated ; and illogical arguments, made to appear convincing. As far as the apologists of Bibliolatry are concerned, they might just as well have the tables of Joseph Smith to deal with as the writings of Paul. If the Mormon apostle had but the veil of extended chronological distance between his person and theirs, the same reckless assumptions, the same special pleading, the same specious casuistry, the same ignorance and plausibility, would suffice to place the Mormon prophet in the seat of Moses. Moreover, if the writers of the Bible had prefaced their books with a distinct disclaimer of special inspiration, — if they had said, in so many words, they were inspired in no higher sense than their intelligent readers, — would the truth they gave us be less the truth, would their ideas be less valuable, would their appeal to the mind and heart be less authoritative? The answer came with the deepest emphasis from one's own experience; for, as the true nature of the Bible became evident, the divine word lost nothing of its beauty and power. As the Messiah is not degraded when found in the form of a servant, the literary Messiah (as it may be called), should not be despised when it is seen to have come in the unromantic fashion of human thought, with the homely drapery of ordinary speech, and through the accustomed channels of inspiration. The answer, also, came from the study of other faiths. I found God had spoken to his children through literatures which, while in every respect inferior to the Jewish and the Christian, contain the same holy precepts, the same elevating ideas, the same aspirations after perfection; flashing from amid absurdities of thought and errors of fact, like the jewel eyes of their own idols from the poorest sculpture and the most ridiculous costume. The Apostle Paul, recognizing their obligation to value and prove faithful to the divine word as it was uttered to them, said, "That which may be known of God is manifest to them; for God hath shewed it to them."

THE SCRIPTURES:
A MONOGRAPH.

" Only then when the grass withereth, and the flower fadeth, — so speaks individual experience, so speaks the voice of history, — is it known assuredly that the word of our God shall stand for ever." — F. D. MAURICE.

"The Bible is a record of truths and observances, of ways of life and ways of worship, handed down from age to age, moulded by each in turn ; growing fuller and richer with time." — DR. TEMPLE, Bishop of Exeter.

"The Holy Ghost is more than the Bible. This should be our teacher of religion; not the dead, earthly, equivocal letter." — NOVALIS.

CHAPTER IV.

THE SCRIPTURES.

THE consideration which finally led me to reject the popular notion of the Bible was the utter impossibility of an enlightened and honest man, in our day, professing to be the subject of theographic inspiration, — whether he should affirm he was the means whereby the very words, or only the ideas, of Deity were conveyed, — and the impossibility of intelligent and holy men believing such a profession. Where could we find a man to affirm this? Would the highest minds of the church? Is it conceivable that the Pope himself could? Could we imagine it of any of our great moralists and philosophers? Who are the men who have made such professions in our time? Are there any above the rank of the Mormon leader, Joseph Smith? What should we say of our best and most gifted men, if they published a book as from God Himself? We could say nothing less than that it was a strange instance of delusion. We know what would be the verdict, if such a man as Robert Hall stood forth, and said, "Here is a book God inspired me to write: so that it is His own word. It contains a history of the ancient peoples of this land; also, proverbs, forms of prayer, prophecies, and letters, all conceived by the mind of the eternal God." Should he protest, in the most solemn terms, against its rejection,—should he affirm, with the sublimest eloquence, the truth of his claim,—his friends would mourn, and his foes condemn.

Was human nature, was human society, different in their essential elements nineteen or thirty centuries ago? Who were the men who wrote the books? Who are the men it is claimed wrote them? Were they more than mortal,—intellectually, indeed morally, did they surpass the greatest minds of this age? Is it in the nature of things, that, in time past, there were a class of men who could believe themselves thus inspired, and of whom it could be believed by their contemporaries, and of whom it ought to be believed by us? What had I been taught of these men from childhood?

The writers of the New Testament, it was admitted, were not only men, but in many respects inferior men. As my pastor taught: "They were not men either of learning or genius. This is sufficiently proved by the writings they have given to us, and is confirmed by all we know of their condition and course of life." "The treasure was deposited 'in earthen vessels,' that the excellency of the power might be of God." "They indicated none of the marks of genius in their works." "They were not, and could not have been, free from the peculiarities of their country and age." "Their prejudices were many and strong." "They were as selfish in their aims as they were narrow in their views." "Though they listened to the wisest and kindest teacher that ever lived, yet, after his three years' ministry, they did not understand his most frequently repeated sayings." "They differ (in their account of Christ) widely from each other, and all of them yet more widely from the great original." "They were ignorant, selfish, worldly, and proud."[1] It is not necessary to admit all this: it is enough for my purpose to see clearly that they were men with ordinary human attributes, and more than ordinary nobility of character; for, if they were not, their opinion of Jesus can be of no more worth than the opinion of some

[1] "The Excellent Glory;" pp. 101 to 110.

"ignorant, selfish, worldly, proud" neighbor in the next street. If such a man should give me an account of any thing, and seek to secure my credence by affirming God had specially communicated it to him, I *must* attribute it to his pride, and not to special illumination. Let me, then, go right back to those early times, and see the thing, as it were, for myself, — see if it be possible for a sane man, in the very presence of these Jews who wrote the Old Testament, the Gospels, and Epistles, to adopt the orthodox theory of inspiration. See if it be conceivable that good men could have sat, with the scroll before them and the *stylus* in their hands, saying to themselves: "I am writing a part of the Bible, — a book which shall be considered as much God's word as if angels bore it fresh from the hand of the Deity. My arguments, God's arguments! my opinions, God's opinions! my recollections of events, God's chosen way of writing history! my compilations of traditions, God's approved method of grouping transmitted, floating information of the past!" But the task was revolting. One shrank from assuming the possibility of such infatuation in men of the sort we perceive the apostles were. If they were ignorant, they were surely men of healthy minds;

if they were liable to err, they must have been men of honest character; if they believed themselves favorites of Heaven, they could not have had such overweening conceit as to imagine what orthodoxy imputes, — that they were expressing the exact thought of God; and, not only so, but expressing his final word.[1]

But I imagined them at their task. As Paul writes a letter to this or that church, in Greece or Asia Minor, is it conceivable, — *has God given me the power, or any one the power*, to believe, in full view of that scene, — that the living, sane, devout man, writing to religious friends counsel, arguments, personal items, as clergymen now write to their churches, ever dreamed he was writing what should have the force of a celestial document, bearing the autograph of the Creator? Or, as Mark writes the substance of the account Peter is supposed to have given the early Christians of the life of Jesus, who can draw near to that evangelist, and imagine himself saying to him, " The Gospel you are writing is God's own account of His Son." I thought

[1] " The authoritative oracle has spoken for the last time ; and nothing now remains but to learn, with what simplicity and humility we may, the true import of the celestial utterances with which we have been favored." — " Hinton's Works, vol. vii. p. 342.

of a representative of popular orthodoxy entering the writer's presence, with his theory of plenary inspiration, saying, " In the years to come, these words you write will be bound up with the Law and the Prophets, as of equal authority. You write just what God would write, if the pen were in His hand instead of yours." What must be his reply, in the very nature of things, if he be neither a fanatic nor an impostor,— if he be a devout, sane, holy man? If assured such would be the fate of his work, could he write another line, or permit what he had written to pass from his hands? He knew, far from every word and sentence being infallibly felicitous, he could not remember exactly every expression of Peter ; nor could the apostles' remember, as the various renderings of conversations and events show, exactly the order of occurrences, the verbiage of conversations, and the details of incidents in connection with the life of their Master. In the immediate presence of the Biblical writers, I cannot think any such claim could be put forth by them. It is as unthinkable as if they claimed God had appointed them an oligarchy to rule the world of nations with the sceptre.

Again, we have no such book in existence as

the Bible is supposed to be. It is given forth as the complete revelation of God to man, forming an organic whole ; that here we have all the writings produced under the conditions which stamp these as God's word ; that the books we have were from the beginning in the sacred collection, and esteemed as highly as they are now. The fact is, we have not all, nor nearly all, of the Scriptures ; that is, the books which were considered canonical by the Jews, and the books which were regarded, in the early ages of Christianity, with as much veneration as those of our New Testament.

On the authority of Emmanuel Deutsch : " The number of Biblical writings that perished must be very considerable indeed. Distinct traces of a great many have survived in our canon. There is, for example *The book of the Wars of Jehovah* mentioned in Numbers ; *the book of the History of Solomon*, in Kings. In Chronicles, we are told of *histories of Samuel, Nathan the prophet, Gad the seer*, as sources for the life of David. In the same work, there are references, for the further history of Solomon, to the *Prophecy of the Silonhite Ahia;* the *Vision of the Seer Jedai* [*Iddo*] *on Jeroboam*. The books of the Kings adduce (more than thirty times) certain annals both of the kings of *Judah and Israel.*" Beside these, there are mentioned the writings of *Shemajah*, of *Jehu*, of *Hosai, etc. ;* the book of *Jasher*, the book of *Enoch.* "Of these productions, great or small (with the exception of the last), there is no living trace now."

Then, in the New Testament, we have probably but a fragment of the writings of Paul. The letter for Laodicea mentioned in the Colossians, and one epistle to the Corinthians, are lost beyond doubt.

Then, it is a matter of uncertainty whether the Epistle to the Hebrews, the Gospel of John, the greater part of the Acts, the Second Epistle of Peter, the Epistle of Jude, and other epistles, were written by the men who are regarded as "inspired." We have, then, but a part — perhaps a small part — of the Bible. And, of that which we have, no unlearned man can be sure what part was originally in the Scripture. As a matter of fact, thousands of people regard Mark xvi., from the 12th to 20th verses, as of equally high origin as the Sermon on the Mount; yet it was not in the original Gospel, but is an addition by an unknown hand. It is a matter of dispute whether the introduction of John's Gospel is genuine.

Nor has there been any agreement among learned men as to what is Scripture and what not. Saint Augustine and the early Fathers made little distinction between the Apocrypha and the other books. Origen and Athanasius insert the book of Baruch; and the latter rejected the book of Esther. Luther was of opinion, that "Isaiah borrowed his whole art and knowledge from David in the Psalter;" "the history of Jonah is so monstrous that it is absolutely incredible;" "The Epistle to the Hebrews is not by Saint Paul, nor, indeed, by any apostle;" "St. James's Epistle is truly an epistle of straw;" "the Epistle of Jude allegeth sayings and stories which have no place in Scripture." As to the book of Revelation, Calvin denounced it as unintelligible, and prohibited the pastors of Geneva from all attempt at interpretation; while the celebrated Dr. Lowth scrupled not to pronounce it a book that either found a man mad or left him so. Erasmus, one of the most learned fathers of the Reformation, rejects Hebrews, Second Peter, and Revelation.

If, then, we are to believe the Bible because of its origin, not one of us will ever have time or scholarship enough to settle what is Scripture, and what is not. While convinced the sacred writers were men like those now on the earth, — divinely illuminated to express truth in the same way ordinary men are to receive it; while convinced they had no monopoly of divine influences; while in no way limiting revelation to one nation or age, — I perceived they were, in an eminent degree, inspired by the Spirit of truth. Their accuracy in recording details is often questionable; their opinions are sometimes fallacious; their narrations of events are often meagre; their conception of truth is in many instances crude: but, it seems to me, nothing can impeach their truthfulness. They were men who wrote, evidently, what they thought was fact. They tell the whole story, whether it reflects favorably or unfavorably on their great historical leaders and saints. We cannot imagine a sect chronicler writing of one of his denominational leaders as the writers of the Jewish histories do of David. Take any life of Calvin written by a Calvinist, and see how the part the great Genevan took in the trial of Servetus is softened down or denied. But in the Scriptures, with divine simplicity the story of David's crimes, or Solomon's licentiousness, is related without disguise or apology, and stands side by side with the records of their devotions. In the New Testament, the same fact is apparent. The apostles' faults are not concealed; their differences, in no way suppressed. There they stand in the Gospels, — brave, noble, holy men, who erred and sorrowed even as other men; and, if the partisan is apparent at all, it is in such a form that we are convinced the writers were unconscious of their prepossession or partiality.

Further, I perceive they were inspired by *the Spirit of righteousness*. They were men, as far as we know them, who aimed at ennobling their fellow-men. The prophetic spirit breathes in their words. No priest has written on the sacred page. Not one of all the millions of ecclesiastics has contributed to the sacred volume. The shepherd, the physician, the fisherman, the king, the tentmaker, have been called from their task to do what we might have expected the priest to have done. Herein is the wisdom of God. In every age, in every church, the clerical mind has been the prey of disease, the victim of oblique vision, the instrument of its party or church. It has been bound hand and foot by subscription, public opinion, and self-interest. Truth has asserted itself in spite of the clergy as a class, not by means of them. The prophets, Jesus, and the apostles need not have suffered, had the clergy been truthful, brave, and self-sacrificing. Christ was crucified because he said what Annas and his predecessors ought to have said. The sacred writers evince that they were, in an extraordinary measure, raised above party, national, and sectarian considerations and influences. Indeed, it is wonderful, that this book, written "by Jews, for Jews, to Jews," is so truthful, and breathes such catholicity that, however antagonistic we may be to Jewish traditions, ideas, and characteristics, we welcome the work of their ancestors with as cordial a gratitude, and read it with as implicit confidence, as though it had been written by men who neither shared their religious preferences, national customs, nor mental and moral constitution. There is nothing an enemy could say with truth of the Jews, but what the Hebrew writers said of them. There is nothing a foe could with truth say in disparagement of Samuel, David, Solomon, the priests, the apostles, more damaging than what is herein recorded. The writers were eminently righteous. They either wrote to raise men from folly and sin, to seriousness and holiness, or else to record the story of the past with fairness and force.

Now I asked, How came these books, in the first place, to be regarded as specially sacred? What is the root-idea of the canon? What must have been the method by which these tracts found their way, first into universal esteem, and, then, into the sacred collection of the Jewish or Christian church? Of the Pentateuch we do not speak: its authors are unknown, and its history to the time of Ezra is wrapped in obscurity. The Jewish histories were probably regarded as sacred writings from the first, because the record of a sacred people.

As far as we know the origin of the Bible books, they could not have become "sacred" writings in the lifetime of the authors.

The prophet must die before he is appreciated, and it is equally true he must have died before his writings could be admitted to the sacred canon. If Joel or Hosea or Isaiah or Jeremiah had taken their prophetic scrolls to the priests, and said, "Our words are from God, for the perpetual enlightenment of the church; admit them to a place by the side of the Law," they would have met with supercilious disdain or priestly anathema. And certain is it, if the evangelists or Paul and Peter had written to the churches, affirming that their works were of equal authority with the Law and the Prophets, the early Christians would have regarded them as insane or impious. The fact is, the writings of the prophets and apostles were read and pondered for long periods,— indeed, ages, I should conjecture. They lay like seed, at first, alone; and, as the influences of reflection, conscience, and piety were brought to bear upon them, their inner meaning developed and grew, until at length the people — the plain, uncritical, devout, unprofessional portion of the people — treasured them for the spiritual help they afforded, without considering the literary defects or historical mistakes they contained, without imputing any specially sacred character to them nor to their authors: reading them very much as vast numbers of Episcopalians read the Prayer-book or the "Imitation of Jesus," and as Protestants, generally, read the "Pilgrim's Progress;" because they speak what is helpful and interesting, — not because they imagine their favorite authors are either impeccable or infallible.

Then the priests, ever mindful of the authority of prevailing opinion, yielded assent to the popular verdict, and officially announced what before had been informally but generally expressed; and so far compromised themselves, in their eagerness to sail with the wind, as to garnish the tombs of the prophets they had slain. The sacred books are the monument of the triumph of rational godliness over priestcraft. It is the divine truth struggling — if I might so say — for utterance through the vernacular of unofficial and natural piety. The ecclesiastical bodies have ever been imposing the externals of religions on the attention of men, — the subtleties of philosophy, the wonders of thaumaturgism, and the obligation of sacraments. The spirit of the Bible is, for the most part, non-ecclesiastical, not anti-ecclesiastical. Its writers were eminently religious men, and accepted very much of the teaching of their church. They did not undervalue the letter: they rather desired to reanimate it with the spirit which alone could give it meaning. Jesus himself never separated from the Jewish Church: for the communion of his birth he, evidently, ever entertained the tenderest and most loyal regard. Paul, in his memorable saying, professed his undying devotion to Israel; and all his writings bear traces of his sympathy with all that was good in Judaism. And the prophets never dreamed of standing isolated from their religion. They sought to transcend, not deny, what was commonly taught. The Bible may be said to be the Eternal Spirit of truth speaking through laymen to the church. It is not the offspring of the church, but the expression of independent, and even revolutionary, piety. In other words, it is not so much the expression of the ecclesiastical church as of the invisible, holy, catholic church of faithful, reason-using men. It is a remarkable fact, that the Scriptures, as far as we know their authorship, were the product of *individuals*, not of societies. They who wrote were not commissioned, authorized, nor even countenanced, by any one. No prophecy nor epistle comes with indorsement of any kind. The prophets and apostles obeyed an inward impulse, stood apart and alone saying what they perceived was truth, and apparently never asking if what they wrote would be in accord with the church's teaching, — the true method, indeed. Truths ever accord one with the other. True intuitions, whether they be granted to Hindoo or Hebrew, are harmonious, — a grand argument for the doctrine of one fountain of light and order. The same Spirit which led these holy men to write their thoughts induced the pious minds of after-times to approve them. They wrote, because they felt their ideas were the truth of God. Men elevated their words to the rank of authoritative statements, because they in their own hearts and minds believed them to be true.

I could now stand, Bible in hand, and say to Science, to Biblical Criticism, to Reason, to Conscience, "Come one! come all! eliminate its errors; we thank you for doing so. Leave no lines which can be proven false, immoral, untrue, or pernicious. We have such assurance that this book contains God's word, that you may take every thing away which was not in the original documents, or which resulted from human ignorance or error, and His truth shall still shine forth as the light. You take but its rags, its corruptible body; but its spirit can never be disproved." I could turn a bold front to every irreverent and immoral sceptic, and say, "We have nothing to conceal. Do your worst to discredit these records. Say, 'It is the writings of Jews, to Jews, for Jews:' so do we. Say, 'It bears marks of human hands:' so do we. Say, 'There are parts of it which give immoral ideas of the Deity and of human relations:' so do we. Say, 'God has enshrined his word in the Koran, the Shastras, the Vedas, as truly as in the Bible:' so do we. And, after all these admissions, we hold up this book, conscious that none can deny our assertions: Herein is the best history of the development of religion. Here we can trace the dawnings of man's idea of God. We open the first page, and find he thought of Him as a Patriarch walking in the evening in a garden, working until fatigued, and then resting. We go on, and find Him spoken of as visiting men in person, and eating with them; then, as a being who regarded a father's slaying of his son as a very meritorious act. We go on and on, and find, at length, the highest ideal of Him, from the lips of Jesus, as the Eternal and Infinite Father."

We see the moral development of the world. Now men are polygamists, and good men imagined themselves blessed of God if wives and concubines were added to their households. Later, we see domestic purity and chastity recognized as the supreme conditions.

We see, in the early ages, God was propitiated in sacred places, by sacred rites; but, in the fulness of time, the truth is perceived that the divine kingdom exists apart from sacrifice or priest or ritual. Such is its historical value, that, as we turn over its pages, hope springs up in our hearts: it testifies the world is growing better! Human ideas are purer, holier! Thank God, Abraham's day is not our day! How would we weep and mourn, if a good man should seriously imagine God required him to take his son to some adjacent hill, and offer him up as a sacrifice! that day is for ever gone. Men cannot any more think so of their Maker. The shadow moves on the dial of time, and, as it moves, man is drawn nearer to God! That history, and all these early histories, should fill our hearts with thankfulness and our lips with praise, that our race is growing upward, that we are finding God. These histories revive the good hope of a golden age: if man has so grown in wisdom and knowledge, to what may he hereafter attain? Think, too, of its salutary and inspiring precepts and suggestions. Think of the quickening and consoling power of the records of God's dealings with the human soul. It matters not who wrote the Psalms: it is enough to know, in the ages past, that men turned to God as we turn, and found as we find an answer to our deepest needs and holiest aspirations. The anguish of David's soul at the memory of his sins is echoed in our own hearts; the sense of pardon and peace he knew comes also to us. The prophets, protesting against formalism and crude theologies, help us to bear witness for God, that it is not sacrifices or oblations he requires, but a pure and contrite heart. Our spirits go back to Isaiah, to Jeremiah, to Ezekiel, to Micah; and we find help and comfort in the thought, that these men of God were bearing, ages ago, the same scorn and isolation we have to bear in our endeavors to purify religious faith and practice. Here we come to the career of Jesus, with his "serene and cheerful piety, his belief in a kingdom when the glad tidings of a restored paradise should come true, his faith in an eternal goodness and love, in the spiritual riches which elevate the possessor above all finite cares and anxieties, in the self-recovering power of the human will, the ability to exhibit outwardly the promptings to a life of saintly well-doing, of meek forbearance, and patient endurance. Exalting, refining, spiritualizing the law, raising it above all trivial restrictions of time and place . . . through the new, expansive, stimulating spirit of his teaching, — he sanctioned a religion of the heart, an internal righteousness; . . . unintentionally, though not always perhaps unconsciously, introducing into the world a principle which ended in abolishing what he sought to complete; till at length the pure and peaceful reformer, awakening the suspicions of the traditional party, perished as the revolutionary opponent of conservative Judaism."

We come to the Epistles, and find what his disciples at the first thought of him. Our hearts respond to their declarations, — that his cross stands for glory, that his love was unutterable, that his character was divine.

We need not say what is untrue about the Bible, in order to get the blessing from it. We need not endeavor to prove that ancient Jewish ideas of God and religion and morality are as worthy as the revelation which comes with Jesus Christ. We need not maintain that there is no revelation from God but that in documentary records, in order to value these records. We need not hold to the notion that the Gospels are specially inspired, in order to appreciate the blessed life there so imperfectly delineated. Religion will not suffer if the truth be told about the Bible, — that religion which consists of a righteous heart and a pure life. But our creeds may be destroyed, our prejudices will be smitten; this ism and that ism may totter beneath such admissions. But a life like Christ's — a life of pure and elevated sentiment, of self-denying love, of holy zeal for God and man — can abide and flourish. Nay more, if all the sacred writings of the world perished, — if we should awake to-morrow and find every Bible gone, and forget there ever was such a treasure in existence, — men would still discern the great fundamentals of religion. For, though the Bible perish, *God liveth;* and He is nigh to every soul that seeks him.

ON FINDING CHRIST.

"Was Christ a man like us? Ah, let us try
  If we then, too, can be such men as he!"
                                    MATTHEW ARNOLD.

"Known and unknown; human, divine;
  Sweet human hand and lips and eyes;
  Dear heavenly friend that canst not die,
Mine, mine, for ever, ever mine:

Strange friend, past, present, and to be;
  Loved deeplier, darklier understood;
  Behold, I dream a dream of good,
And mingle all the world with thee!"
                                    TENNYSON.

CHAPTER V.

I. HOW I FOUND HIM.

COMING to Jesus Christ, in my case, was like waking up slowly from a dream, in which the person seen distinctly in the one, is seen indistinctly for some time in the other, process. At first, there was much confusion, arising from the different conceptions which have in all ages prevailed concerning the person of Jesus. The traditional Christs differ the one from the other as much as the traditional Peter and John. And as the painted representation of apostles might be mistaken in some cases for their Master, so the intellectual ideals run the one into the other. I saw such a conception as that of the Broad Church school was as far from the conception of evangelical revivalists, as the Madonna of Murillo is from the Madonna of some inferior carver of wayside shrines. Every party, every sect, cries, Do you believe in Christ? meaning thereby, not all that is on record concerning him, but that fiction, more or less faithfully constructed from original materials, which is to them Jesus. I found that belief in him meant belief in their notion of him. One might say any thing in *accord* with that conception of the original, as one would conceive it at first hand; but nothing of a conflicting character. One must know the evangelical ideal-Christ, and then study the Gospels; for, if we should study the Gospels first, our estimate might be widely different. Evidently, the church Christs were one thing; the Christ of primitive Christianity, another: the church Christs having, no doubt, the general features of the beloved Master; but his images stand flooded with the pyrotechnic splendors of sacred romance, or bedizened with the tawdry of ignorant and passionate devotion. There is, evidently, a Roman Catholic at the heart of the Roman Catholic Christ: just as there is a Protestant at the heart of the Protestant ideal, and a revivalist preacher at the centre of the Christ of revivalism. We should not have hesitated to attribute diverse and contradictory notions of Jesus to Catholics. To me, it was plain the same was true of Protestants. There is, as in the Roman Hagiographa, a general character pervading these ideals of the Master; yet they differ so radically from each other that distinct persons might have been their prototypes. The series ranged from Jesus, the simple peasant prophet, connected in some mysterious way with Deity, to Jesus, the only God; and, in a descending scale, far beyond the lines of the church, to Jesus, the over-rated reformer. The Pantheon seemed crowded with images, so various in form and comeliness, yet all bearing the name "Jesus," that I left them all, and read the Gospels, as best imagination could help me amid the scenes of Galilee and Judea, asking, "Who art thou, Lord? What should we have thought of thee, had we known thee as we know our contemporaries?"

Is there a basis, in fact, which redeems his worship from the guilt of idolatry? Of course, we tinge all our conceptions of others with our own personality: no wonder there are lords many and gods many called by his name! But was there something in him which would revolutionize all natural interpretations of his person and work? Was there that in him which would lead the holiest and most intelligent of the ministers of the Christian religion to do what is ascribed to the Apostle Thomas,—fall at his feet, and say, "My Lord and my God," in the orthodox sense? I was conscious there was nothing in me which would rebel at such a prostration and ascription, if I were only sure it was right. Full often, indeed, the charm of his name, the admiration of what was unquestionably true of him, and the longing to join the familiar ecstasies of my religious kindred, tempted me to suppress inquiry as to his rank in the universe, — to be rational everywhere but here. But the thought stung like reproach: "What! worship, without being sure you worship God! Worship a Perhaps! Honor Christ so little as to adore him as God, when, if one knew the truth, it would appear such worship would be to him blasphemy deep as the worship before a pagan shrine!"

A diviner being than Jesus (in the sense I imagine Paul thought him divine) is to me inconceivable; that is to say, if what I think he was, of whom the Gospels speak, be true. Then, if I could be an idolater, it would be at his feet. Unutterable beauty radiates from the face looking through the time-obscured lattice of the New Testament. There is none like him. There he stands always: young, dauntless in his advocacy of the right, firm in witnessing to the truth, daring the worst a fanatic age and a bigoted priesthood could do, without a trace of vanity or vulgar scorn. Sweetness and grace, force and chivalry, wisdom and kindness, are all combined with an intensity and harmony unparalleled. Socrates would have bowed here ; Plato, Confucius, would have done him honor, could they have known him as we see him. And his cross, — nothing stirs, subdues, enthralls like that! Dead at thirty-two, — dead, because those lips disdained euphemisms ; dead, because that broken heart could not dissimulate, half-state, seem to agree ; dead, after receiving nothing from the world more than millions of lifeless souls receive ; dead, after giving all he had to give for the upraising of his fellow-men ; dead, Jesus, the pure, the noble of thought and aim, the self-sacrificing benefactor! Dead at thirty-two : one's heart is in his grave as one thinks of it. Yet if he, revered and glorious as he seems to me, — if his cross stood here, and he turned those dying eyes on me, saying, " I am the equal of God ; I am the second person in the Trinity," — ought I to believe ? ought he to expect it of me ?

My thoughts went back to Nazareth, — to those early days when he and his mother went to the house of God together. There they sit, beneath the same roof. What, if one of our ministers of the Christian church had mounted the reading platform of the synagogue, and addressed him as they address him now,— as the Divine Being! If a Trinitarian had preached there as they preach now, unfolding to him the doctrine of the nature of God as formulated by Latin Christianity, do I not know — just as I know he was good — that he would have looked with eyes flaming with wonder and anguish? I thought of that suffering face, of that lowly, unambitious soul, of that devout, adoring nature, sitting there, while learned demonstration should be made that he was the Maker of heaven and earth; able to tell us the deepest secrets of the universe; able to say what his subjects were doing in the planets and stars,— God! God eternal, immense, immanent, immutable, omnipotent! It was anguish to realize such a scene. It was plucking truth out of flames.

Or to bring the scene nearer. I imagined a modern congregation. The organ swells; the choir chants; the hymns, the prayers, the sermon, all relate to his absolute Deity. There sits his mother in that pew beside him, and her children and her husband. And Jesus rises at the close, saying, "All is true. I am God: I am the second person in the Trinity. Joseph was not my father. I walked on water literally, and did all you hear of me. This body rose up from the grave, and went up to heaven." Could we believe *that man*, looked he as noble as Christ indeed must have looked? Could he — could a mortal — do any thing so strange, so mysterious, so wonderful, as to make it *right* for me to say, "I believe thou art the Deity"? "Yes," a million voices answered from all Christendom! And I answered back, "You think so of one living in the shadowy past! But *could* Jesus be believed if he came now and here by *you*, and made such a claim: walking the streets of Boston; standing here in this place; born an American instead of a Jew; named as we name men; his hands horny with work done in one of our shops; his form clothed with raiment from our looms and factories?" Nay, such a claim would eclipse every virtue he possessed, every wonder he performed, every act of mercy he had wrought; and Love herself, ready to enshrine him in her heart of hearts, would weep above his grave as one unfit to retain her devotion; and Malice would write the true and cruel epitaph, BLASPHEMER, while none could protest, and few would pity! Nay, Christ was too divine to claim Deity; and, as a matter of fact, none of his contemporaries ever entertained such a thought; and his immediate disciples were too intelligent, too Christ-like, too pious, to think of his deification. That took place among the class, and by the methods, substantially, which exalted Mary to the rank of a goddess, and the saints to that of subordinate gods; which gave us transubstantiation, the commercial theory of the atonement, purgatory, and auricular confession. Having gone carefully through the New Testament, examining the proof passages of Trinitarians, I found no satisfactory evidence that Jesus was regarded as Deity in his day. Indeed, there is abundant proof he was *not appreciated* even by those who loved him best. But, if all the passages Trinitarians claim could be accorded them by just criticism, would not their very presence *be fatal to the credibility of the records;* if their writers and those they report were so superstitious as to regard any being as identical in personality with the Eternal? If Christ, present here and now, ought not to be believed if he claimed to be God, surely no book should be believed that claimed it for him.

At the same time there can be no doubt the apostles taught he was the Son of God, — the Messiah; the incarnation of heavenly wisdom, love, and truth. To Paul he was the Messiah of the Jewish hope, — the Saviour of the world from sin and ruin ; to John, the incarnation of the eternal Logos, which had been immanent in humanity, and now was incarnate. Yet, whatever their mode of expressing or accounting for his glorious and excellent nature, they ever spoke of him as one endowed with a kind of higher self such as others possess. "We are partakers of the divine nature, heirs of God, joint heirs with Christ." Peter, amid the thrilling ecstasies of the day of Pentecost, spoke of him as "a *man* approved of God among you." Paul constantly called the holy nature in Christians, "Christ in us."

Plain, rational, as all this appeared, a dread rested on me lest I might be mistaken, — lest I had called the light of a dream the light of day, and confounded fancy with fact. Yet, the reflection silenced fear, " *We have to do with* JESUS. If he be the Supreme One, he would not be angry with a man for candid, honest inquiry, and frank declaration of conviction about him. Man or God, he was too noble to be offended thus!" At the same time, at first I so far lacked vividness of insight into the inestimable dignity to which the human character may attain, that I felt as though the Lord stood discrowned and disrobed and disenthroned. My fears spoke of disloyalty to Christ, of treason with a kiss against my spiritual king, — aye, of blasphemy against my God. I remember saying in bitterness, " Let me go back to the gods of my fathers. A man cannot live long, cannot be very certain of any thing. Error, if error it was, was kinder than thou, Truth, if truth thou art." Many a mournful day passed. Pope Tradition menaced me and the spirit of the Past seemed to say, "Art thou wiser than thy fathers?" Knowledge and inspiration and courage came at last, — bought at a dear price, but not too dear. I ventured to think the comparison admissible of the mule, which in some countries strikes with its hoof among the spines of the cactus, and drinks, with lamed foot and bleeding lips, the few drops of milk which ooze from the broken thorns.

The strengthening thought was this: "Do you love him less who died for man, because his rank in the universe is not supreme, — because the divine nature dwells in him, rather than the divine personality? What! did he, as Paul teaches, regard deification a thing not to be reached after; and must you mourn it was not his condition?" I said at length, — indeed, at once, — " I am capable of loving and serving God in the man Jesus Christ, though to all eternity he be as poor, as despised, as suffering a servant and son of the Father." And I chanted in my heart the old and faithful saying, "Who shall separate us from the love of Christ? Shall tribulation, or distress, or persecution, or nakedness, or peril, or sword?" Let the labors and agonies, the malice and the woe, he endured here be repeated there, I would call him Lord, and account it an honor to share his shame. I felt this in my soul, the more I meditated, as I saw him, as it were, descend from the altar before which from childhood I had bowed in adoration, — as I saw ethereal and celestial pageants fade away, and he standing there, alone, in the homespun garment, a living man, saying, "Follow thou me." I felt a reverence deep as my former homage was ecstatic. The question now arose, "Is the Christ of idea a higher and more beneficial conception than the Christ of fact? Does the Christ of the church present a nobler embodiment of moral excellence than the Christ of history? In other words, is Christianity better than Christ? Ought we to preach the one, or the other, or both?" I reflected as to their comparative eminence. It was not necessary for me to decide: but, rather, it became me to bow before the Author of all, in thankfulness, that there is both the Christ of poetry and of fact; that whatever Jesus may have thought of himself, whatever he considered his mission to have been, whatever his design, — he has given rise to the holiest and noblest series of moral portraits the world possesses. And could he pass from home to home, seeing even the crudest pictorial representations of himself; suggesting to the rude and humble peasantry of Catholic and Protestant countries thoughts of one better than themselves, of self-sacrifice, of divine compassion, of undying love, — he would not think he had lived in vain. While shocked at the enormous priestly follies and pretensions alleged as maintained by his authority, it would be, perhaps, more than a compensatory consideration, that, to the great masses, the influences of even the exaggerated and fantastic portrayal of his character has been an immense and abiding source of help and consolation, and has been eminently corrective of the cruel and oppressive presence of priestcraft and its terrors.

At the same time, it was evident that truthfulness demanded we should distinctly distinguish between the ideal and the real, for the benefit of those capable of appreciating the difference. I saw that the apotheosis of Jesus was desirable for the many, who are incapable of duly appreciating virtue when it is in their midst and on speaking terms with them. Few, like the Master, could discern the exquisite piety of the widow in casting her mites into the treasury. Virtue, glorious to us when suggested by the saintly form looking down from the cathedral window, is hardly noticed as it does the same thing represented of him in the home or in the street.

But while the ideal Christ is necessary to many, — is, indeed, *more* than the real could ever have been, — it seemed to me most obligatory to govern the imaginary by the actual ; for around the former has gathered, and is gathering, such a wealth of myth, legend, impossibility, and idle speculation, that its original beauty is constantly growing less discernible ; and in some instances so obscured is it, that some other name than Christ's would better become it. Yet, I reflected, Happier far are those content with the lowly original, the divine in humanity, the grace and truth connected with a mortal and suffering life! The church, unconsciously no doubt, has not been content with her Master as she found him : she took off his homespun, and clothed him in purple and fine linen ; she was dissatisfied with his plain speech, and imputed to him her theologies; she saw not the grandeur of his pre-eminence as the first among his brethren, and therefore made him a god, built him a shrine, gave him a priesthood, and invested him with the better attributes of Jupiter and all the gods. Nor did she stop here. He had poor relations: there was simple, motherly Mary standing in contrast with her bedecked and enthroned son. Mary, too, must be crowned and deified; and then her mother and her husband, and all who stood near them: so that to-day the rough, unpretending fishermen of Galilee appear in ten thousand instances with fine clothing, such as they never could have worn if they had lived till now; and with faces fair and poetical as they may have dreamed the angels have. The real Christ could hardly go, and in his own person evoke a reverent glance, where the ideal is most adored. Jesus of Nazareth would disappoint. He would come to his own again, and his own would not receive him. Surely, blessed are they who can keep his memory fresh, and see him as he actually was; so that, if he returned and lived his Judean life over in verisimilitude, with the exception of the national and local peculiarities of his former existence, they would be to him all that the family at Bethany was.

II. WHAT HE IS TO ME.

Of Christ, I believe, all the Scriptures clearly teach; but I distinguish between what is established testimony concerning him, and what is yet in dispute. Of the miracles, I need not speak; holding, as I must, the simplest word of truth he spoke, and the least noticed act of compassion, are greater proofs of his divine mission and character than walking on the sea, or raising the dead; just as, if he came now, I should feel his patience under insult was more divine than his walking on the Atlantic from England to the United States. I distinguish, too, between platforms from which he is viewed and described. Standing on these by the speakers, I say as they said.

Among men of common attainments, unused to special phraseology and exalted modes of reasoning, I say with Peter, "Jesus of Nazareth, a man approved of God among you by miracles and wonders and signs which God did by him, in the midst of you, as you yourselves know." Standing with the Apostle John, or whoever wrote his recollections of Jesus, speaking after the writer in a dialect of Oriental philosophy,

I can say, contemplating their conception of the Eternal Logos, "In the beginning was the Word, and the Word was with God, and the Word was divine." And then, contemplating the holy character of Jesus, I can localize and see impersonated this oft-manifested Logos, and say in him, "The Word was made flesh and dwelt among us; and we beheld his glory, the glory as of the only begotten Son of the Father, full of grace and truth." Standing with the Apostle Paul in view of all the yearnings of Israel after their highest moral ideal, seeing in the Messianic hope of a Redeemer, as one says, a predication, not a prediction, of the truths Jesus taught and embodied,—I can say, Jesus "is made manifest" "by the scriptures of the Prophets."

But we are not living in times when Oriental philosophical conceptions and phraseology are understood; therefore, if one asks me, "Was Christ man or God?" I say, "Man." We are not living in times when the nature of Jewish ideas is commonly apprehended; therefore, if one asks me, "Was Christ predicted by the prophets," I say, "No." But in neither case do I give my conception either of his nature or rank or authority. Among those who can understand me, I can say, "Jesus is the Messiah, the Son of God, the Lord, the Mediator, the sacrifice for sin, the elder brother." But to the masses I must say, "Jesus was a man approved of God among you." The more exalted phraseology is the efflorescence of philosophic thought. Apart from higher insight into spiritual things, these phrases become a source of confusion and superstition; and have borne the deadly fruit of idolatry, as in the popular error of the Deity of Jesus. In surrendering this doctrine of Christ's Deity, I do not surrender the fellowship of the apostles. It appears to me, Jesus was the signal instance of humanity. No thought, no ascription, no doctrine, which has been conceived by those of the apostolic age, who understood his character, seems inadmissible. The fatal error which has deformed post-apostolic Christologies has been the isolation of Jesus from humanity. The apostles, whatever they claimed for him, recognized that the same attributes belonged to others. Did they say he was divine, that God was in him, that in him the Deity was revealed, that he was the son of God? They also said, "Ye are heirs of God, joint heirs with Jesus Christ;" "Now are we the sons of God." Did they say he was the Lord? They also said, "Submit yourselves to one another." They spoke of him as Lord in the sense of the elder brother, — one of themselves, though first of all. Did they speak of his meritorious death? They also insisted, "and we ought to lay down our lives for the brethren." Did they point to his wonderful life, and its beneficent influences? They drew the conclusion, "As he is, so are we, in this world." But, since then, superstition has drawn a barrier between him and us. It studied his life as though it was not the most conspicuous specimen among many, but the *only specimen* of its kind known to man; until at last he is separated from humanity, and openly addressed as a being of another order. Instead of "the first begotten," he has become "the only begotten." Instead of seeing in him the highest possibilities and noblest expression of our nature, they see in him an object of wonder and awe, like that which ancient mythologies described. The key of all Christologies is found when we apprehend these facts. What is discovered in Christ, however glorious, is what to some extent exists in every good man. The church has stood engrossed before Christ, like as ancient Greeks might be imagined before the Apollo Belvedere, expatiating on the form, expression, and influence of the statue; until the idea was lost that each one of them, however imperfect, was represented there; until it became blasphemy to say the physical nature, if not the physical perfection, typified was their own.

The church has lost the knowledge that we are members of Christ; that all that she says with truth of him is a symbolical exhibition of the relations of man to God, to each other, to virtue, to vice, that we may come "to sit together in heavenly places with Christ Jesus;" that what he is we are or may be; what he did we are doing or ought to do. For example, Christ is the MEDIATOR between God and man; not an agent reconciling two who are hostile, but bringing into harmony two who are separated by the ignorance, guilt, and indifference of one. Even so should we draw men into accord with our heavenly Father, by persuasion, by the presentation of worthier conceptions of Him, and truer expositions of the heinousness of guilt and frivolity. Is he an INTERCESSOR? So is every man holier than others: his soul goes out in sorrowful and yearning aspiration for the return of the profane and world-absorbed to God. Is he a KING of saints? So, in proportion as men are holy, they give law to less sanctified but appreciative natures. Was Christ's death *a sacrifice* for sin? We are "crucified with him." In our degree, devotion to the will of God, to truth, to righteousness, produces such a moral effect that men are saved from sin and drawn to self-sacrifice. In like manner, the doctrines indicative of the relations of Christians to Christ are true of their relations to each other. For instance, the church insists, as did Christ and his apostles, on "*belief*," ascribing to it salvation. We can believe in Christ as we can believe in no one else, because of the eminence of his worth. We can believe wholly in him. But in so far as men are like him, so far we can believe in them. He who believes in righteous men; who welcomes the word of God as it speaks from their virtues; who feels the responsibility of life in presence of the fruits it bears in others; who comes to hope for humanity at large, encouraged by individual moral triumphs and achievements; who finds in their company stimulus to high endeavor, — is saved with an everlasting salvation, — saved from sin, despair, and unserious living. *The union of believers with Christ* is the harmony of holy souls with their pattern, their ideal, and their inspiration, — a union of the same kind as that they enjoy with contemporaries. So of the accidents of his life, whether revealed in historic prose or in traditional poetry: every life has its immaculate conception, — the Eternal Spirit communicates to the human the divine; every life has its obscurity and its ministry, its transfiguration, its Gethsemane, its Calvary, its death in darkness and shame, and its resurrection in life and honor. As the apostle taught, we are dead with him, and risen to sit with him in heavenly places. Our lives are framed on the same pattern. Say, "He is the Son of God:" it is also written, "Now are we the sons of God." Say, "You are but a man:" it is also true, "He was a man, the son of man," the most natural of us all, and therefore the more divine. And, as to his teaching, I accept it as I believe he would have men accept it. Not that I understand all he believed; for this is impossible, seeing we have but meagre memoranda of his discourses and conversations. Nor is it clear we understand his exact meaning in every particular in the sayings which have come down to us. I find he himself asserted that his first disciples, while honored with his confidence and immediate friendship, but imperfectly understood him. Nor would I regard it as obligatory on me, living in this age, to adopt the same symbolism he found in common use and employed. But I believe in *him*. I believe his consciousness of God was profound and clear; his relations with the Father were transcendent; his character was the most eminent instance of human excellence, — was an embodiment of all the prophetic preachers of righteousness had conceived in their moral ideal, — a man whose spirit was unfalteringly devoted to truth and righteousness; who combined outspoken honesty and intrepid boldness with meekness, gentleness, and humility; who was single of purpose and self-sacrificing in all his course.

As to the Gospel of Jesus, I regard it as the restatement, in simple preceptive and illustrative forms, of the best ethical teachings of mankind. I cannot believe he intended to originate a new theological system, however legitimate it may be to construct one from his sayings. It seems to me, he took the fundamental ideas of the religion of his times for granted, seeking to infuse new life into them, while he endeavored to remove the accumulated superstitious accretions of ages. The method of his instruction, and the audiences he selected, sufficiently demonstrate the unambitious nature of his mission, as he himself regarded it. He confined himself to oral teaching, — to conversations and sermons. We have no treatise, however small, from his pen. We have simply *memorabilia*, handed down by disciples not skilful in literature nor eminent for exactness as reporters. From these we know many of his opinions and the principles underlying them; but we do not know, and probably never shall, the dogmatic belief of Jesus. As Bunsen, in his "Hidden Wisdom of Christ," observes, "The doctrine of Christ cannot be known as it ought to be, until two problems shall have been solved. In the first place, some additional light must be thrown on the last pre-Christian development of Judaism, and on its connection with Christianity. In the second place, a satisfactory reason must be assigned for the mysterious fact, that the first three evangelists have evidently agreed not to refer to any of those important sayings of Christ which have been recorded only by the beloved apostle, whose Gospel was not published before an advanced period of the second century." It is incredible that Jesus intended to originate a theology in this way, seeing nothing requires more exactness of statement. We all know the radical difference between what Calvin taught and what Calvinists now imagine he taught. As

Sir William Hamilton remarks, "Nothing can be conceived more contrary to the doctrine of that great divine than what has latterly been promulgated as Calvinism (and, in so far as I know, without reclamation) in our Calvinistic Church of Scotland."[1] If this be true of a theological system originated within the age of printing, and written by its author, we cannot be in doubt as to what would be the fortunes of a theology communicated orally, reported long after, and handed down for centuries in manuscripts.

The audiences of Jesus were for the most part unlettered people. The glad tidings he delivered must have been something which, in his judgment, the simplest could receive. None but philosophers can understand philosophy; and none but theologians can appreciate theology. A special education and intellectual aptitude are necessary in both cases. It is a reflection on the wisdom and manliness of Christ to suppose he addressed the lowly peasantry of Palestine with the intention of introducing, through them, a theological system, or instituting a new ecclesiastical church. When the wisest, the profoundest, the noblest, of our theologians consents

---

[1] "Discussions in Philosophy and Literature."

to gather around him the ignorant peasantry of England or Germany, with the intention of making them the apostles of his peculiar system of thought, then, and not till then, let us impute such a course to him of whom we know nothing but what is worthy. As I understand it, "Jesus Christ came into the world to save sinners;" to bring men moral aid; to awaken the conscience, to inspire the best affections, to introduce the soul to nearer intimacy with the divine. He saw humanity harassed with intellectualism or besotted with superstition; he denounced alike the Scribe and the Pharisee, and told mankind to be righteous rather than to theorize about righteousness, to love God rather than to propitiate Him. His was the divine voice without, in precept, sustaining the divine voice within, of conscience and reason. The common people heard him gladly; for he spoke the words which emancipated their best selves. Their hearts answered to his word; necessary conviction gave authority to his affirmations. He left the field of controversy and the museum of theories far behind, and spoke to the heart of the things which were sure and eternal, — of duty, of peace, of obedience to God, of love to man. His was the sublime mission to witness to the truth,

. purged of the extraneous, the accidental, and the erroneous. No prophet has arisen like unto him; for all others have complicated eternal verities with temporal opinions, and obedience to God with artificial requirements. Whatever Christ's philosophical and theological system may have been, whatever his respect for established religious cults, whatever his use of received dogmatic symbols, — his Gospel was a simple appeal to the heart to obey the highest law it could know, and follow the purest ideal it could conceive. He seized on the truth, — on incontrovertible certitudes, — and preached these to the multitudes.

To sum up all : I bow not to the authority of the church, nor of its literature; but to the authority which was before them, which speaks within them, which speaks apart from them, — *that* in the soul which perceives spiritual truth. Therefore I bow to the authority of Jesus Christ; for in him I recognize what I should myself have announced as the will of God, had I arisen to the height of spiritual elevation he attained. And this must be according to his mind. "Never do you hear Jesus employ words which come to this, — 'What I teach you may be absurd, but believe it because I teach it.'

Far from that, his method, his constant method, consists in acting on men's consciences in such a way as to lead them to acknowledge the truth of what he says." [1]

[1] Dr. A. Reville. "Progress of Religious Thought in France."

THE RECORD OF A TEMPTATION.

"Woe unto him that saith to the wood, 'Awake;' to the dumb stone, 'Arise, it shall teach!' Behold, it is laid over with gold and silver, but any breath is not in the midst of it at all." — Hab. ii. 19 (Dr. R. Williams's translation).

CHAPTER VI.

TEMPTATION.

AFTER it became clear to me how erroneous are current notions concerning the Bible, the origin of the church, the theories of salvation, and other dogmas of speculative theology, I was still hopeful of finding a way by which I could conscientiously remain somewhere in the evangelical ministry, if not in my own church. Before me were examples of clergymen of the most unimpeachable piety, sincerity, and outspokenness, who remained in the Anglican communion, with ideas of the church, its sacred literature, and its theology very similar to my own. There were, too, in the Congregational and other churches, eminent and excellent men who continued to use the old symbolism, while they insinuated, gradually and indirectly, into the minds of their hearers, those very truths of liberal thought, which, if they had been openly and directly taught, would have caused the most violent opposition. I asked myself if, in view of all the facts, it was not a kind of duty to accept, and use as far as possible, the old ideas and phraseology,— to lay the ghost of prejudice by familiar language, and pacify bigotry by using its shibboleths? After all, was not the attachment of the masses to the old theology, and its influence on their real beliefs, greatly overrated? What Robert Hall said of formal creeds might surely be said of all: "When they cease to be the subject of dispute, they have become antiquated and obsolete." If they were never called in question, would not these dogmas be as harmless and uninfluential in relation to the spiritual life as Utopian sociological theories when confined to philosophers and contemplative philanthropists are to social life? Would the citizens of Alexandria, of Constantinople, or of Mecca, have been the worse in any respect, if they had never heard of the controversy which rent their cities asunder, and made men glare on each other as fiends incarnate, because they held opposite theories of the generation of the Divine Spirit. At the time it was deemed all-important, as much so as any theological dogma dividing the churches now. "Every corner, every alley, of the city was full of these discussions,— the streets, the market-places, the drapers, the money-changers, the victuallers. Ask a man, 'How many oboli?' he answered by dogmatizing on generated and ungenerated being. Inquire the price of bread, and you are told, 'The Son is subordinate to the Father.' Ask if the bath is ready, and you are told, 'The Son arose out of nothing.'"[1] Would the good men and women of the world be less religious, less philanthropic, less happy, if they had never heard of the clerical statement of theories and facts which we call creeds? What are they but signals for strife, rallying points of organizations, party cries, which are magnified into importance by the mystagogues who have made theology their sole study, until it dwarfs every thing else, and by the priests who beguile the people with the idea that belief in these opinions is bound up with their eternal welfare? *But they are in existence;* a fictitious value is attached to them. Let them be assailed, and men who really care nothing for them in times of peace are ready to die for them in times of conflict: just as men fight for a sovereign simply because he is the king, — their king, — when revolution seeks to establish a better government; whereas, in the times pre-

[1] Quoted in Stanley's "Eastern Church."

ceding war, the majority know little of his personal character or administration. Is it not the best thing to let them alone? They are potent only when their potency is denied. The fetich of the savage, we know, does him neither harm nor good; but seek to pluck it from him, and he curses you as if you had blasphemed the divine. Why should I not leave these literary fetiches alone, and be content to let those who prize them think I also value them, if so be I can do them good by my silence? Good men, on all hands, evidently draw their strength from the indisputable and underlying truths of natural religion and practical virtue,— the most sectarian even. What does it matter that they attribute their spiritual well-being to belief in this or that dogma? So that a man is well, why need the physician assure him that the medicine to which he ascribes his health were disguised bread-pills, and that he will continue to be just as well without them? Let him take them: it is better he should be deluded on this subject than flung into a passion, and led to doubt the wisdom of his doctor's advice on all subjects. My belief was unchanged as regards the truth beneath the creed. I could honestly say, in some sense every article of it was the divine word. But if I spoke out, and said frankly, that popular and ecclesiastical theology were obsolete and undesirable symbols, I should not be credited with belief in any real sense, and the opportunity to serve and enlighten my own denomination would be gone. Within the fold, it seemed, more could be done to immediately liberalize men, than without. As a minister unsuspected of heterodoxy, my word would be far more acceptable than as an avowed opponent of the theological fashion of the sect. Broad Churchmen, in my judgment, have done far more toward reforming historic Christianity[1] than rational dissenters. Within the church, known and loved by one's followers, the truth is less likely to be rejected, than from an alien, unknown, unloved, practically impersonal. Within the church, men know that your interests and theirs are bound up together; know that you must desire the prosperity of their order; and, above all, believe you in sympathy with them on far more subjects than those you dissent from. You may be even deemed "heretical on some points:" still you are a brother. Then, the reformer is less liable to extravagance in denial, less tempted to vio-

[1] Although I do not think they have done as much toward placing religion on its final basis.

lence in the use of language, less impatient of ignorance and bigotry. It is a family affair: both parties are controlled, softened, and disposed to hear opposite statements of the details of belief, by mutual affection. Could not the revelation of ideas be brought about best by a slow, cautious, gentle method; by a noiseless changing of each separate item of belief? It has been done to some extent. The old theology of the Independents has glided into that of modern Congregationalists, without any violent shock or startling innovation. To secede from my denomination was like surrendering it into the hands of traditionalism. Would not this be a guilty disregard of their highest interests, if, instead of being alone, I had found like the prophet the thousands who were like-minded? Yet was my duty as a witness to the truth less imperative than it would be if accompanied by numbers? Would it therefore be right for me to remain where I was, and go on teaching in the old way? Taking refuge in the thought, that persons of insight, those having a genius for religion, would see through the haze of ancient statements the underlying simple truth, while ungifted and unspiritual minds could not know much more of divine things than they do now, whatever the form of expression; that if we taught a religion to the masses at all, must we not expect that, to the majority, our most refined ideals will be fetiches; that, by the same ignorance and perversity, our purest symbols were deformed, misapprehended, the majority of people were incapable of distinguishing between a denial of gross symbolism and a denial of the truths they rudely indicated? Were not they responsible for their superstition, and not we? Were we to blame if our illustrations became dogmas, our panorama actualities, our signs the truth itself? Moreover, might not our ancient imaginative doctrinal system be a sort of overstatement or exaggeration absolutely necessary for mankind in its present condition, like fairy tales or object-lessons for children? Was not nature full of illusions; and did men care, or was it desirable, they should think and speak with scientific correctness of phenomena, even when they knew the truth; as, for example, men know the sun does not rise and set, and yet nature does not cease to maintain the illusion. Exaggeration in some departments of truth is necessary for educational purposes; as, for instance, minute things must be magnified. A fly is not seen as fully in its natural size as when magnified under the microscope. Does imaginative Christianity do for the historically remote and the ethically transcendent a similar office, for those whose spiritual vision is dull,. or whose lives are too engrossed in the practical for contemplative thought? Could there be a standard symbolism which would mean to all what it meant to the studious and refined? Was there any objective thing or subjective idea which meant the same to everybody? Was not all popular instruction incorrect; and must it not be, as long as men were too busy or uncultured to appreciate the difference between truth and its statements, facts and that which is said of them? The traditional apparatus had all the advantages of familiarity; if it was cumbersome, antiquated, and worn, it was at least acceptable. Although we know a worthier and more truthful mode of conveying ideas, it was practically useless, because unintelligible. Ought we not to speak in the *patois* of a people incapable of understanding our own purer dialect?

Had it not been the order of Divine Providence? Were not men taught religious truth and duty, at first, by such revolting symbols as human sacrifices, childish rites, painful ordeals, cruel captivities? Did not gross symbolism become refined as the people became civilized? Had not religious teachers become more spiritual in the same proportion as the people became more intelligent? Had not the demand always determined the supply? Had God ever forced purer forms of truth on unprepared hearts? If I said to the people, "The simple truth about the sacrifice of Jesus is the moral influence of the surrender of his will to the will of the Infinitely Perfect," should I not be as unwise as a man who, in the days of Solomon, had stood amid the temple services, and declared the Levitical dispensation was provisional, — that it was simply an elaborate mode of teaching the simple duties of a holy life?

Had God's way been the way of my conscience? There is nothing apparently wrong to him in the slowness, the exaggeration, the illusion, and the gross symbolism which have marked the religious development of the world. Is not the esoteric mode of thought a correspondence to the divine silence? God leaves the world, as it were, to find out gradually better things, even as he leaves the individual to seek after the truth. Is not this spirit which clamors for frankness and accuracy a fretful, restless, morbid tendency, born of pride of insight and impatience of restraint? Does it not do harm? Does it not destroy before we are able to build? True, such a course would be called "lying" by the people for whose good it is resorted to, if they found me out; but, then, their ideas of moral distinctions are as gross and inadequate as their conceptions of dogma. It seems lying to me, I reflected; but, having found how erroneous traditional definitions are, might not lying itself admit of such a restatement as to exclude from its category of instances consciously expressed misrepresentations of truth, presumably resorted to in the interest of religion? I remember reading about this time Newman's "Apologia." It reminded me that the deepest and best minds had allowed the necessity of what is popularly regarded as lying, in some cases. Paley said, "There are falsehoods which are not lies; that is, which are not criminal." John Milton: "What man in his senses would deny, that there are those whom we have the best grounds for considering we ought to deceive, — as boys, madmen, the intoxicated, enemies, men in error, thieves? I would ask, By which commandment is a lie forbidden? You will say, By the ninth. If, then, my lie does not injure *my neighbor*, certainly it is not forbidden by this commandment." Samuel Johnson: "The general rule is, that truth should never be violated. There must be, however, some exceptions. If, for instance, a murderer should ask you which way a man has gone." Jeremy Taylor: "To tell a lie for charity, to save a man's life, the life of a friend, of a husband, of a prince, of a useful and public person, hath not only been done at all times, but commended by great and wise and good men."

Might I not, I reflected, bring myself, by legitimate processes, to do that which, in the vernacular of the people, would be known as "lying" for God, for humanity, for the truth's sake? Might I not grace His altar with a dog so faultless, that it would be accepted?

But, in better moods, I began to suspect myself of throwing these ratiocinative sops to a disquieted conscience. For it was clear to me, in my nature, real as the consciousness of being was that which said, "If you had no personal interest to serve, would you contemplate this connivance at error, and take such pains to prove it lawful? Does not this very reasoning denote 'the clerical mind,' as it is called; the priest practising upon himself; vested interest going to the shrine of error, with a gagged conscience in its train, and the banner of truth flaunting above its head, to conceal its nefarious purpose, and to disguise its impious selfishness?" I felt the imperious presence of something stronger than logic in my soul, which said, "Prove the church has lied! Prove emergencies demand falsehood! Prove wrong is right! Aye, prove the Eternal permits evil! *You* must not lie."

If reason were convinced, conscience never could be. Whatever excuse could be found for others in such a course, I ought not to find any for myself, but must live in obedience to the law of my being. Whatever I might think and feel in speculative moods, in practical life I should know all the sufferings of an accusing conscience; my holiest enjoyments would be interrupted by the inward whisper, "accomplice of error!" and my efforts to inculcate truth in such a way would be paralyzed by the fear I was an impostor. The practical outcome would be self-deterioration. Such reasoning was as available for vice as for error. Vice might be shown in the light of exaggerated virtue. Murder, for example: what is it but a coarse and brutal manifestation of self-regard or indignation; its more refined form, hatred: as the Apostle John taught, "He that hateth his brother is a murderer"? Therefore, if I had a congregation — say, like the Thugs of India — who were murderers of the worst kind, if my living depended on their support, I could by the same esoteric method of thought justify a similar exoteric approval of their vice. I could quiet conscience by the reflection, "Seeing the root-idea of murder is proper self-regard, murder is but a vicious or gross form of duty. My congregation could not appreciate this virtue in higher forms of its expression. If I denounced their practice of destroying life for the purpose of avenging wrongs or securing advantages, I might undermine their proper sense of self-regard, and weaken the legitimate desire of self-advancement. Does not the Creator permit one race of beings to prey upon another? Do not all men, in the sense John used the term, 'murder' their fellow-men? The difference between my congregation and others is, they adopt a coarser method, they slay the body by violence: others slay reputation and peace by insinuation. Surely, if proper self-regard must overstep its boundaries, — and it would seem a human infirmity, — it is better for men to be honest and speedy in their action, until they can be cured of the propensity. If I should at once educate them out of bloody deeds, done at rare intervals, would it be possible to give them such an elevated conception of proper self-regard that they would refrain from the more refined, more frequent, and more malignant forms of murder?" Grotesque as this illustration must seem, it reflects the shape in which self-reproach assailed me. It derided the method of reasoning into which I had fallen,—that method by which the worst errors of religion had been fostered, the method by which thoughtful men had ever been seduced into compliance with superstitious dogma. I had read enough of church history to know, that the curse of the ages of ecclesiasticism had been its delusive casuistry, its timorous reticence, its spirit of compromise in the face of emergencies, danger, and vested interests!

I came at last to a recognition of the fact, that error had as permanent objectivity, as definite outline, as vice; and that both were as real as material phenomena. The same mystical process whereby the facts of error and vice lost their substantiality, rendered the outer physical world impalpable, impossible, delusive. I perceived that all human ideas, whether of the physiological or physical, were inadequate; that from higher planes of consciousness the soul finds itself utterly alone, where nothing appears as it does ordinarily. Where man sees what he can never express in words, what if he tries to express will be unintelligible to all save those who have had the same vision, there he is simply a wonderer. Mind, morals, matter, float beneath him, like ever-changing and intangible clouds; the affairs of men are a distant scene; the weight, the form, the reality of every thing is gone. Nor would we slight such vision; but seek, rather, for clearer light. I thank God for it, as for an unspeakable gift; for in those weird and oppressive regions or moods, where fancy strove to delude conscience, availing itself of one's wonder and inexperience, there was felt the presence of the Infinite, — the nameless but supreme fact, from whom came hopes and trust unutterable; in the dialect of human language, hopes of an eternal unity, —

> "One God, one law, one element,
> And one far-off divine event
> To which the whole creation moves;"

when error and truth, vice and virtue, may appear as shadow and substance: so that the suspicion of Dualism shall for ever flee away, and God may be all in all.

I saw that the condition of practical usefulness was sympathy with the current conceptions of things, physical and spiritual, of my fellow-men; that the speculative tendency must be controlled; that it was my duty to think less apart, and more with the race; that I ought to fulfil my part in the plane of existence on which I found myself. They who have known this experience will understand the thankfulness with which the sense of worldliness returned, and the joy with which one tasted and handled the good word of life as spoken in common things, — in daily mercies.

The difficulty was now resolved into a question of simple truthfulness. I had to choose, not between indefinite and transcendent abstractions, but between the familiar forms of truthfulness, or connivance at error. It was, manifestly, my duty to be truthful about theological and religious matters as about political and secular affairs, — as truthful as a conscientious witness in a court of law; not only so exact as to escape an action for perjury, but always as exact as when it is to one's personal interest to tell the truth: testifying to matters of fact with candor; relating opinions with modesty; treating religious legends, myths, and allegories with the same respect as those of non-sacred literature.

Again the question arose, Whether it was not possible to be severely truthful, and yet complete my ministry among my life-long friends? It was a revolting thing to conclude the contrary. The faces of so many whose character must ever be admirable in one's esteem — men whose honesty I can never doubt — occurred to me. What! can these be truthful, and not you? Are these at liberty, and you bound? After all, did not the rational preponderate over the imaginative in Baptist theology? Was it not possible to be silent when accordance was impossible? Was any individual so responsible for denominational errors that it became his imperative duty to sacrifice his ecclesiastical home? If I were a heretic as judged by its dogmas, I was a loyal adherent as judged by its principles. Was there not a higher duty than heeding the admonitions of a sensitive conscience, a higher duty than immediate testimony to the truth as I saw it, — the duty of remaining to help on the emancipation of the denomination from within? Others — many others — might be thinking as I was thinking, and in God's time might we not come together, and be the leaven which should influence the whole lump, completing what the fathers began; making the Baptist denomination absolutely free from Romish dogmas, and in fact, as it has been in name, the champion of unqualified religious liberty? Perplexed, fearful of premature action, wishful of remaining among my friends, the resolution was well-nigh formed to correspond with the men I venerated, and had known from childhood; stating the whole case, and asking for their advice. But the purpose was arrested. The simple avowal of disbelief in the current doctrine of the atonement rent a gulf between us. They could not counsel with me as a brother beset with difficulties; no answer could come from them but expostulation. If they thought with me concerning traditionalism, they dare not intimate as much. They would have placed themselves in my power: the publication of such a letter would have been their ruin. They could not write, and say, "Believe as you do, but remain." For, whatever they may think, if they continue where they are, they must seem to approve. Though Christ himself should speak out of heaven to one of them (as Paul saw him in vision), saying that their theological theories are crude and obsolete, they could not hope to remain; but one of two opinions would prevail: either falsehood or else insanity were added to heresy. If, on the other hand, they were, as I believe they are, sincerely in sympathy with orthodoxy, why need I write? for I know their answer beforehand. They will mourn, protest, warn: the case is too far gone for discussion. They would entreat me to repent, as one denying the Lord. To write to them would be an act of self-deception, — a folly inviting resistance, bidding for obstacles, calling on denominational pride, piety, and compassion to intercept my secession from their ranks.

But, again: was I the victim of my reading, or of some obscure mental disease? If so, they might help. The thought was dead as soon as born. "I know I am right" (I reflected); "this consciousness of the possession of truth concerning Christianity and religion is unlike what I knew before. I am as one who has come up from a mine into daylight at noon. Mystery encircles all I know; but within the circle things are distinct." Egotistic as it must seem, still I say it with deference, that my conviction was of that nature, that it was more reasonable to suppose the denominations of evangelical Christians wrong than my conclusions; just as I know it would be more reasonable to suppose the whole Catholic Church errs concerning the meaning of the Lord's words at the Last Supper, than it would be for me, alone, to conclude as anti-sacramentarians do concerning their import. The unreasonable in Christianity has but two factors which the unreasonable in daily life has not; viz., antiquity and wide-spread indorsement. Liberal religion would have no battles to fight against the speculative and imaginative side of Christianity, if every man now living had lived from the days of Jesus. Then it would be seen that every thing which contradicts reason has no more authority than preposterous propositions from our neighbors. Whatever a philosopher or theologian affirms now is accepted on the ground of reason. If any one should say, "This I announce is a new theory, or opinion of truth; but it is unreasonable," who would listen to him? It is true, unreasonable speculations are advanced. Still, they are accepted on the ground of reason. It is a foregone conclusion that the orthodox creed is eternal truth, and every thing must harmonize with it; that is, must commend itself to the human reason as in accord with these ancient statements. Modern theology must be reasonable, — in accord with its antecedents and with our sense of truth. But these antecedents were not always ancient or in existence : they must have been ventured for the first time once. Was, then, the duty of our ancestors different from ours? did it behoove them to accept what was palpably unreasonable? If it was ever right to accept unreasonable creeds, it is now right to accept unreasonable new creeds. All that is necessary for the proclamation of a new and erroneous religion, if it is to be based on the same principle as belief in the irrational part of orthodoxy, is for men to assert their notions are from God, and a sufficient lapse of time, — say two hundred to a thousand or eighteen hundred years. In other words, the unreasonable in religion owes its hold largely to antiquity. "Now, for the truth of things, time makes no alteration : things are still the same they are, let the time be past, present, or to come. Those things which we reverence from antiquity, what were they at their birth? Were they false? time cannot make them true. Were they true? time cannot make them more true. The circumstance, therefore, of time, in respect of truth and error, is merely impertinent." [1]

[1] John Hales, in "Rational Theology in the Seventeenth Century."

The other factor is, *Unreasonable things in religion are believed by a vast number.* It seems shocking self-assertion to affirm, "I am right, and myriads are wrong,"—among them one's fathers and pastors. Even David, when he says "I am wiser than my teachers," repels us. But (one reflected) can I shift personal responsibility to the multitude? Can I leave off protest and dissent right here, and say, "Henceforth I believe as the multitude"? It is not in a conscientious man's power: truth is truth to him still; falsehood is falsehood, let him say, let him vociferate, what he will. There was no power in earth or heaven, as long as Galileo's mind was unimpaired, which could make him believe contrary to the facts he had ascertained concerning the solar system. The determination of what is true and what is false rests with a higher power than ourselves. It is beyond me, it is out of my jurisdiction, to dismiss a conviction at the bidding of all the world. To me, some facts of the spiritual and historical realm which militated against conventional belief were as self-evident as the material forms of nature. Surely there was no help. I must deny God in me, in conscience and reason, if I would remain where I was. But two courses were open: to try to deliberately deceive myself, or else live in conscious deception of others. The emancipating thought came at last, giving force to all other considerations, "*If I had only God to deal with*, would there be perplexity?" If there were no congregation waiting to hear its own opinions; if, unimpressed by historic, ecclesiastical Christianity, with its venerable traditions; if there were no legacy bequeathed to me of euphemisms, disguises, sophistries, and falsehoods; if one had no care for reputation, nor dread of anathemas, nor shrinking from the misjudgments and expostulations of beloved friends; if personal interests and ambitions did not hang in the balance; if free from superstitious fears, doubt of courage to dare all consequences; *if I had only God to consider, if I had only to be loyal to the voice within,*—would there be any difficulty in deciding my course? It cannot be worthy in His sight for me to go on saying, in solemn terms, directly or indirectly, "I believe Jesus, the prophet of God, is God Himself." It cannot be right to say, or to seem to say, "I believe the blood of that holy man appeased His wrath," in any sense. I would not dare affirm it of a holy man, that he was vindictive as this implies. Nor can I, in His holy presence, go on saying, or being supposed to say, that the highest virtue is agreement even with His perfect mind, when men know nought of Him but in part. Nor can I teach that the end of our life is to seek a better fortune in the future. When most impressed with His unspeakable glory, one is ready to look Oblivion in the face, renounce all hopes of other and further life, and say, "It is enough to be for one life, to know Thee, the Perfect and Infinite, and then know nought for evermore."

REST AND RE-EQUIPMENT.

"Grant to my heart made lowly wise
The spirit of self-sacrifice;
The *confidence of reason* give;
And, in Thy light of Truth, Thy
Servant let me live."
                                    WORDSWORTH.

"That the basis of religion must be personal, and not traditional, does not mean that the personal element need be so nakedly scientific as to exclude feeling or devotion; nor even does it mean that the traditional is of no value; only, that it does not stand alone." — ROWLAND WILLIAMS.

CHAPTER VII.

REST AND RE-EQUIPMENT.

REVIEWING, finally, the course pursued and the conclusions reached; standing amid the wreck of former opinions; about to be branded as a heretic; misunderstood by even the intelligent; scorned by many, and pitied by those who loved me most,—I began to count what was clearly saved and gained, and to attempt a formal statement of the basis of my religious belief. One's spiritual life, whatever its depth or quality, was unchanged, save in one regard,— there was more of hope in its experiences. *Sin* was the same odious fact: definitions of its nature, theories of its consequences, had changed; but the thing itself remained, branded ever as that against which all the forces of the soul should launch themselves with unrelenting violence. The indwelling Spirit remained ever crying with our spirit, "To him that overcometh will I give;" ever quickening, consoling, reproving. The need of prayer, of watchfulness, of obedience to the inward voice; peace in trust of God, joy in moral triumphs, sorrow in defeat; love for the souls of men, longing to serve and save them from sin and its consequences,—had suffered no alteration. The Cross was still the centre about which one's heart revolved; not as a human sacrifice appeasing the wrath of God, but as a spectacle of self-sacrificing goodness,—a man offering up his will to the will of the Father; silencing every worldly and selfish desire, that he might do for the truth, and thus for the world, what he had come to see was his duty. And this, I saw, was not an exceptional act,—not heroism under the stimulus of tragic excitement, but the culminating triumph of a life of self-abnegation for the truth's sake. Indeed, The Cross glowed with new meanings; came nearer and nearer, until one's heart grew reconciled to all the sorrow and shame awaiting a public confession of different belief. God has set Christ in the midst of the world, it seemed, that men, in shaking off antiquated religious errors, in order to testify to the truth as they find it, may not be afraid of the names they who do this have to bear.

Instead of personal piety becoming less, it became more, imperative and precious. Let me say this with much diffidence, but also with deep emphasis; because, I find, it is assumed by many of our orthodox friends that such conclusions as mine can only be reached by men who are dead to that inward life which they teach begins with the epochs called "conversion" and "regeneration." It is distasteful to speak of this; yet it is surely a kind of duty for me to say, I know what is meant by "inward experience," as the term is used among evangelicals; and solemnly testify, that experience in my case has known no other change, amid these changes of opinion, than could be accounted for by a purer conception of the object of worship. The same life is mine as when the world was to me the palace of a Celestial Despot, and when God might prove a Torturer at last. The scene is changed,—*so far* am I. The world is "my Father's house," and God is the Father. As one whose lot in the world is changed from dungeon to home, so am I changed: there are fewer ecstasies of woe and joy, a more even but far happier life. One has passed from the sublime in Tragedy to the sublime in Peace. There is no loss here. Amid the grander world now seen, with higher conceptions of spiritual things, one's reverence is deeper than it could have been before. With the loss of revered ideals and familiar associations, one's heart is driven to seek states of mind in which the divine realities come without word or image or sensuous thought.

But better than this testimony is the fact, that no higher type of saintliness prevails than what I find in the biographies of rational Christians. This is said and reiterated, because once I did as others are still doing,—deny piety to the adherents of absolute free thought.

Now, as to substantial gains:—

1. I have *freedom from intellectual confusion* as regards religion: all that is knowable is coherent and reasonable. What is discernible is self-consistent. Mystery is around all knowledge; but knowledge is that from which mystery has receded,—in other words, it is the revealed.

2. *Liberty of thought.* The privilege of thinking naturally,—of perceiving spiritual things with one's own eyes,—of regarding truth and error, the probable and improbable, as I needs must if faithful to the powers God has given me.

3. *Discernment of the underlying verities of religious thought.* They are to me facts: it is no effort to believe them; it would be an impossible effort to disbelieve them, as to disbelieve in the reality of simple material forms.

4. *Conscious sympathy with all good men.* For, I perceive, all are inspired by the same truths, and aiming for the same high things. Instead of sending missionaries to those of other religions, to give them primary truth, I would send them brethren, who, valuing their religious systems at their true rate, would suggest to the most pious and intelligent what we believe are higher and better symbols or modes of expressing the simple truth inhering in all religions.

5. *Unassailable hold of the Bible.* What it is to me, it can never cease to be. I take it for its truth, and not on the ground of its authenticity or origin. Should it prove to have been written by Aztecs, or any strange people, or should it be transformed entirely by transcription and other vicissitudes of ancient literature, it matters not. As far as its annals agree with known historical data, or bear the complexion of probability, so far are they valuable; as far as its myths and allegories are illustrative of

truth, so far are they precious; as far as its religious teaching is perceived to be in accord with the reason and conscience of mankind, especially with my own, so far is it the word of God for my guidance. Orthodoxy has no Bible yet, in the sense it claims the Bible is the revelation of God; nor can it ever be sure any text or line of the sacred writings is genuine, until the last deliverance of antiquarian philosophers, philologists, theologians, and Biblical critics is given. Discoveries are being made, constantly, which show whole chapters formerly regarded as the word of God are spurious, or at most apostolic traditions. The Bible, as far as they are concerned, is in litigation,—it is a case in court. It is like territory every inch of which is contested in the interest of various clients; and they are like those who build on ground to which their title is not established. They have had, and may have again, to pull down the costliest structures. Practically, God is silent, and this revelation is involuntarily represented as a questionable relic of antiquity. Yet plain people are expected to receive all these ancient writings as from the Deity, just as they stand, while none of them have emerged from the sphere of controversy.

6. *Deeper consciousness that God is the living God.* That which is, is as near, as energizing, as enlightening, as in the ages gone. To me it is a greater truth that God is, than that His word is; for, if His word spoken in the past were irrevocably lost, He would still be nigh to reveal the truth to our minds.

As one has said, to whom I owe more than words can express, —

"Is Thy breath quenched like a wind that is gone by; or do the children of men live by any life save thine?"

"Is Thy sceptre fallen, and Thy everlasting throne cast down; and are there no more mercies left in Thy treasury?"

"Shall the spirit that is within us strive in vain; and is there no more answer of life to our prayers?

"I heard the voice of the scoffer and the scribe; and they scorned my belief in the *living* God.

"When the earth was young, they said God blessed it; but all things are grown old and darkness is on the world.

"There is nothing now as then: let us speak the words of old time; but not seek the truth now, for it is no more.

"So the scoffer and the scribe spake scorn of Thy children; they set bounds to the Almighty, and counted years for the Eternal.

"In my distress I had said even as they.

"Then I said, 'Blessed be the Lord God of Israel, and of all our fathers, even He that liveth for ever; our souls are not farther from Him now than the first man on earth!'

"I have seen thee, O my God! with the eyesight of the mind; I have heard Thy name like deep melody without sound.

"Thou sendest forth Thy thought in man's heart like the light upon the earth: Thou bringest Thy counsel to pass through a thousand generations.

"Let the Hebrew unrol his volume, and I will learn; but let the Gentile praise Thee, and I will join their songs in Thy name."[1]

7. *I have also gained the liberty of free speech.* One has no longer a case to make out, an inherited opinion to defend at all cost. There is nothing to conceal,—no need of cautious statement or half statement; no concern to prove Christ is in accord with Christianity. My mind hears him from before the origin of the Christian church. There is no motive for

[1] Rowland Williams's "Life and Letters."

rejecting the office of the critic: if he should prove Christ did not utter what before had been ascribed to him,—if that utterance contains the truth, it is the same to me whoever said it. If alleged incidents of his life are disproven,— even if the historic Christ faded from view,— the Christ, the ideal exemplar, the embodiment of perfect manhood, might still be contemplated.

As to the next question, *What is the basis of my religion?* It is "personal, not traditional." It is what God enables me to perceive of Him, not what others have said He is. Philosophy and theology, in their relation to individual insight of divine things, are similar to physiology and psychology in their relation to perception and self-consciousness. They classify, express in symbols of thought, and generalize from what man intuitively and experimentally knows. The consciousness of God is a sentiment of the same kind as the consciousness of our own existence: neither can be verified; neither can be established by logic. If the one is an assumption, so is the other. If the one is evident only at intervals, so also is the other. If we fail to retain a uniform consciousness of the Divine presence, we also sleep. If but a part of mankind perceives God, only a part is awake to higher self-consciousness. How many men live and die without feeling the pressure of mystery as they say, "I am"! They are to themselves what God is to them. They never *sink* into themselves, nor *rise* to Him. Theirs is mainly an exterior life,—automatic, instinctive, mechanical. The same happens to us when we analyze self as when we scrutinize the fact—God! We lose ourselves: we reach limits of thought at last, beyond which is the blackness of darkness; as truly as we are tempted to doubt the Divine existence, we are tempted to doubt our own. If the consciousness of God can be dismissed as a mystical sentiment, incapable of verifying its own base, so ought personal consciousness. No man knows the ultimate fact of his being; no man has seen himself as he is beneath his physical, intellectual, and moral qualities, any more than he knows the ultimate fact of Deity. In the same sense we say, "No man hath seen God at any time," we may say, "No man has seen himself at any time." The two questions stand from age to age unanswered, though persistently repeated, "Who is the Lord?" "What is man?" We cannot symbolize our deepest thought. All we can say is, "I feel He is," "I feel I am." Yet these feelings or intuitions, express them as we may, have all the force of mathematical demonstration, and are as self-evident as phenomena to him who feels them, in the hour he feels them. But, in social life, our ignorance of self and of humanity beyond certain limits does not preclude utterance and accurate knowledge within these limits. All we know, apart from self-consciousness, of man is classified under four heads,—the animal, the intellectual, the emotional, and the moral. These are his attributes, not himself. In like manner, we see the attributes of Deity. In the outer circle is the manifestation of *power*, of ever-living energy: the physical universe appears to us as much an expression of Deity as animal functions are of man. But we also see a correspondence to our *intellects:* in history we trace results which come from remote causes, from the fusion of activities which originated in nations and individuals far apart in point of time and place; we see laws above human control which for ages were not even discovered; we see an element in the conduct of the world which defies human interference, and which compels human co-operation. The highest manifestation of Deity is the moral: beyond that symbolism is impossible. Here is the brightest image of His glory,—that which the Gnostics idealized in the *Zoe*, the *Pleroma*, the *Logos*, the *Charis*, the *Aletheia* (the Life, the Fulness, the Word, Grace, Truth). We see these divine attributes shining forth from all history and from all men. Yet I know this is not all. The Infinite Ego, if I might so say, is as inscrutable as the finite ego. But even as, in my intercourse with man, I come to *him* himself, not to impersonal attributes, — even as our spirits touch by means of these manifestations, while I know not his spirit as He knows it, while I know my own only within limits, — so we commune with God as He is, by means of these manifestations. We approach Deity by the divine, as we approach man by the human. We do not know Him as He knows Himself; but we know Him in the same sense that we know each other.

Every man has an innermost being where no other human eye can look, and an innermost he cannot penetrate himself; yet we know and love and serve each other. And just in this sense God is known and unknown. All that is expressible of Deity to me may be called "Perfection:" all I can conceive of myself, all I am not, — myself freed from limitations. I began: He was from everlasting. I die: He lives for evermore. I am weak: He is omnipotent. I am limited on all sides: He alone is free. I am sinful: He is sinless. I am subject: He is regnant. I am time and space bound: He dwells in eternity, is all and in all. I am dependant, aspiring, expectant: He is the source of strength, the bestower, the goal. Deity is the ineffable answer to humanity, — that without which it is incomplete. I speak of Him as a person, because I cannot conceive of His being at all save in this mode of existence. If I knew of something more worthy than human personality, I should feel it my duty to think of Him after that symbol. But I do not mean that He is such an one as I. am. The idea is absurd to me, because creaturehood seems inherent in the idea of humanity. When I say, after John, I partake the divine nature, I refer to the highest manifestation of Deity, — His moral attributes; or, rather, that in us which is the source of moral attributes, — the Spirit of God. I speak of Him as a Father: for all virtue is paternal, providential, hospitable, helpful, pitiful, satisfying, eternal, energizing. For what He has done, that which has sustained and blessed mankind, that He does for me, resembles more than any thing else the kindness and justice and care of the ideal Father. All that makes the sum of the idea, "*father*," when I reckon up His attributes, makes the same total. The father among us is the one being who awakens and answers to the filial instinct. God is manifested as all this, in what he does and is to us.

Hence the necessity of prayer. It is the outgoing of the soul after the Infinite Alter Ego; it is humanity seeking completion; it is the filial seeking and finding the paternal; it is weakness seeking Infinite Strength, not as a possession, but as a refuge; want appealing to that in which all fulness dwells; imperfection in quest of what it lacks; estrangement, waywardness, incorrigibility, yearning for such harmony with the Best, the Perfect, the All-wise, — that the soul can say, "I and my Father are one." Prayer is answered only in proportion as the will is submissive to righteousness; prayer is consummated only as we come into conscious union with God. The acts of prayer are a child's appeal for the Father; but its spirit is that which impels the whole nature forward, bringing it into loving, peaceful, grateful rest in the arms of Infinite Perfectness and Love. Prayer-words are nothing if they are but requests for certain specified advantages: they are only *prayerful* when they herald the soul's quest for nearer relations with the Highest and Holiest. The language of the truest saints of every age and church has been, "We ask no gift, — as though thou hadst forgotten any thing: we seek Thyself." Yet the prayer for rain, for healing, for fortune, may convey the same holy aspiration as prayers unconnected with superstitious expectations: as filial sentiment, when it asks of the Father the foolish or impossible or inevitable, is nevertheless going out after its correlative. Whether the child has an adequate or inadequate conception of his father, he satisfies the yearning of the filial nature by speaking to him: whether he says, "Take care of me," thinking that, unless he asks, he will not be beloved; or, "I know you care for me," assured that, though he were dumb, he would be provided for.

Here, then, after fifteen years spent in intense sympathy with evangelical theology and church life, I found myself separated from both, by strong and carefully formed convictions: finding the truth of the prophet's words, "O Lord, I know that the way of man is not in himself; it is not in man that walketh to direct his steps;" and that saying of Jesus, "Howbeit when he, the Spirit of truth, is come, he will guide you unto all truth." I could choose obedience to the truth; but could not say what should be truth to me, and what error. A power, not one's self, but immanent and beneficent, had surely led me on from ignorant content with inherited errors to fuller light. The joy of emancipation balanced the sorrow of separation. Whatever could befall, I had the priceless possession of established conviction in most matters of religious belief. The perils of scepticism were passed. My great concern, henceforth, must be to avoid the spirit of dogmatism, by cultivating a broad, teachable, and amiable temper. With controversy or brawling assertion I was determined to have nothing to do. The truth came to me by personal study and quiet reflection; so could it come to others. Further, to use this new-gained liberty and light for the benefit of others, to be a helper of their souls from the thraldom of irrational fears and absurd superstitions, to point them to the true *summum bonum*,—a holy life; to the true source of inspiration,—the God and Father according to Jesus Christ; to be as a "nurse," to use Paul's figure, rather than a sacred policeman or legislator, for the souls of men. One sorrow more than all else distressed me, as the crisis of formal declaration of a change of belief approached : the simple, untheological friends who had profited by my ministry must be plunged into a painful state of wonder, dismay, and apprehension ; and they who had intelligently followed my teaching would remain behind without a religious teacher of the liberal faith, — objects, perhaps, of suspicion, if not of aversion.

The step was taken. To my great regret, all the religious papers of the sect who were requested to publish a statement of the nature of my newly formed views refused, — even those to whom I had contributed most, — so that friends at a distance could have no idea where I stood. Liberal Christians, however, on all hands, wrote words of congratulation and encouragement. Hope revived, that there was still a place for me in the Christian ministry. That place was found in the Unitarian ranks. I came here, saying, "I desire to teach the duties and hopes of men, as they seem to me, with liberty to speak the truth on matters of theology, sacred history, and Biblical criticism, regardless of all consequences." With such a claim my services were acceptable.

The opinion of the recent convert can be of little weight concerning his ecclesiastical relations; but this may be said, whatever importance should be attached thereto, that greater freedom than that existing in Unitarianism is inconceivable to me in any permanent human organization. It is broad enough for the narrow; and purer forms of orthodoxy, *minus* the spirit of fanaticism and bigotry, may be heard within its ranks. I desire not the kind of liberty which is intolerant of conservatism, or which would insist on new symbols and recent discoveries in the realm of spiritual truth, to the exclusion of what is ancient and established. Nor do I desire the spirit which spends itself in shouting for liberty, as though liberty were the only good thing; much less for the spirit which, in its eagerness to proclaim the recent results of learning, behaves irreverently in the presence of learning itself, — the free thought which assumes to pronounce judgment on obscure and difficult problems, without the capacity and information necessary for such a task, — or the free thought which is associated with a flippant and superficial nature. Happily, there is that liberty in the denomination which permits the smiting of every intolerant disposition whether it be conservative or radical, which is alien to the spirit of piety or intelligent freedom. I thank God, after these years of unrest and conflict, that there is one part of the religious world, whatever its traditions, fortunes, or prospects, where the reverently rational can speak the truth fully, somewhere, if not everywhere, within its borders.

" Iter hac habui."

Cambridge: Press of John Wilson & Son.

THE "NO NAME SERIES."

THE GREAT MATCH.

"The 'No Name Series,' in course of publication by Roberts Brothers, Boston, has been a success from the beginning. 'Kismet,' a Nile Novel, is not alone a charming love story, but one of the best-written travel-fictions in our language; and 'Dierdrè,' the longest and best-sustained narrative poem that has been published for a long, long time, also has added greatly to the popularity of the 'No Name Series.' We now have 'The Great Match,' another volume, to be characterized rather as a thorough New England story than classed among American novels, very few of which are worth reading. The author has shown no small ingenuity in making a great match of base ball the foundation of this pleasant and effective narrative. Base ball (facetiously called 'Our National Game,' albeit only an adaptation of the English 'rounders') is elevated in this story into an active element of amusement, connected with which are the incidents which, adroitly worked up, complete the plot. If any one wishes to witness a well-foughten game of base ball, without the crushing, the dust, even the danger (for the ball sometimes hits the spectators and damages their features), let him read 'The Great Match,' and he will learn all about it. This is a hearty, lively, simply told story, another decided hit in the 'No Name Series.'" — *Philadelphia Press.*

"Is a satire on the small interests, great excitements, and petty jealousies of small towns, typified by Dornfield and Milltown, easily recognized by the reader as two of the pretty towns on the Connecticut River. The event of the book, the only event, is a base-ball match, but out of it grow several love affairs. Summer visitors, the affected youth spoiled by European travel, and the thin, learned Boston girl, come in for a share of the author's overflowing and good-natured satire. There are touches of real wit, of artistic taste, and of a genuine love for nature and all true and sweet things scattered through the story, which has strong internal evidence of being written by 'P. Thorne.'" — *Boston Daily Advertiser.*

"We have derived as much amusement from this novel as from any that has as yet appeared in the series. The humor is exceedingly clean-cut, and is, moreover, without exaggeration. The satire is keen, but good-natured, and the tone is healthy. If we are not mistaken, this book will enjoy as large a popularity and as wide an appreciation as have attended any of its 'No Name' predecessors." — *Boston Saturday Evening Gazette.*

One volume, bound in cardinal red and black.
Price $1.00.

Our publications are to be had of all booksellers. When not to be found, send directly to

ROBERTS BROTHERS, Publishers, Boston.

THE "NO NAME SERIES."

KISMET. A Nile Novel.

Opinions, generous tributes to genius, by well-known authors whose names are anonymous.

"Well, I have read 'Kismet,' and it is certainly very remarkable. The story is interesting, — any well-told love story is, you know, — but the book itself is a great deal more so. Descriptively and sentimentally, — I use the word with entire respect, — it is, in spots, fairly exquisite. It seems to me all glowing and overflowing with what the French call *beauté du diable*. . . . The conversations are very clever, and the wit is often astonishingly like the wit of an accomplished man of the world. One thing which seems to me to show promise — great promise, if you will — for the future is that the author can not only reproduce the conversation of one brilliant man, but can make two men talk together as if they *were* men, — not women in manly clothes."

"It is a charming book. I have read it twice, and looked it over again, and I wish I had it all new to sit up with to-night. It is so fresh and sweet and innocent and joyous, the dialogue is so natural and bright, the characters so keenly edged, and the descriptions so poetic. I don't know when I have enjoyed any thing more, — never since I went sailing up the Nile with Harriet Martineau. . . . You must give the author love and greeting from one of the fraternity. The hand that gives us *this* pleasure will give us plenty more of an improving quality every year, I think."

"'Kismet' is indeed a delightful story, the best of the series undoubtedly."

"If 'Kismet' is the first work of a young lady, as reported, it shows a great gift of language, and powers of description and of insight into character and life quite uncommon. . . . Of the whole series so far, I think 'Mercy Philbrick's Choice' is the best, because it has, beside literary merit, some moral tone and vigor. Still there are capabilities in the writer of 'Kismet' even higher than in that of the writer of 'Mercy Philbrick's Choice.'"

"I liked it extremely. It is the best in the series so far, except in construction, in which 'Is That All?' slight as it is, seems to me superior. 'Kismet' is winning golden opinions everywhere. I have nothing but praises for it, and have nothing but praise to give it."

"I have read 'Kismet' once, and mean to read it again. It is thoroughly charming, and will be a success."

One volume, bound in cardinal red and black. Price $1.00.

Our publications are to be had of all booksellers. When not to be found, send directly to

ROBERTS BROTHERS, Publishers, Boston.

www.ingramcontent.com/pod-product-compliance
Lightning Source LLC
Chambersburg PA
CBHW022017220426
43663CB00007B/1113